Policing

SAGE COURSE COMPANIONS

KNOWLEDGE AND SKILLS *for* SUCCESS

Policing

John Grieve
Clive Harfield
Allyson MacVean

SAGE Publications
Los Angeles ▪ London ▪ New Delhi ▪ Singapore

SAGE Publications Ltd
1 Oliver's Yard
55 City Road
London EC1Y 1SP

SAGE Publications Inc
2455 Teller Road
Thousand Oaks, California 91320

SAGE Publications India Pvt Ltd
B 1/I 1 Mohan Cooperative Industrial Area
Mathura Road, New Delhi 110 044
India

SAGE Publications Asia-Pacific Pte Ltd
33 Pekin Street #02-01
Far East Square
Singapore 048763

British Library Cataloguing in Publication data

A catalogue record for this book is available from
the British Library

ISBN 978-1-4129-3542-5
ISBN 978-1-4129-3543-2 (pdk)

Library of Congress Control Number Available

Typeset by C&M Digitals (P) Ltd., Chennai, India
Printed in Great Britain by The Cromwell Press Ltd, Trowbridge, Wiltshire
Printed on paper from sustainable resources

contents

part one
introduction

1.1

introduction to your course companion

In recent years the study of policing has attracted an increasing amount of interest from a variety of academic perspectives: criminology, sociology, social policy and public administration, politics and governance, criminal justice, social history, law and human rights. There are wider tangential interests. Policing as a concept of social control may be of interest to philosophy students. The contribution of policing to foreign policy may be of interest to students of international relations. Press or dramatic representations of policing may well be of interest to media and cultural studies students. Policing can be studied as a sub-set of any of these disciplines or in its own right. Offered at an increasing number of higher and further education institutions, the relatively recent academic specialism of police studies has yet to define a common and traditional curriculum and the permutations of academic modules around policing-related subjects are numerous. That variety and this broad academic community are reflected in this volume, which aims to provide the reader with a general introduction to various key aspects of police studies that may feature in any of the curricula for the above disciplines.

A volume this size cannot hope to discuss in detail the complexities of these different key aspects, but it does draw attention to the breadth of the subject and it will highlight for students of one discipline how other disciplines might be engaged. For those specifically studying policing, this book aims to provide both a broad introduction and a framework for study revision. Its features, explained below, are intended to facilitate this and the book is structured accordingly. Following this introduction, Part Two outlines key aspects that are likely to feature in any policing curriculum. Part Three, based upon the work of David McIlroy (for whose assistance the primary authors are very grateful), presents guidance on core academic skills. In Part Four, additional study resources are presented.

Good practical policing demands a multitude of skills and an open mind, whether the primary purpose is the investigation of crime or the preservation of the sovereign's peace. It often requires the ability to multi-task. It is perfectly possible, for example, for students to focus on police powers purely from the perspective of criminal law and procedure, but such a focused and forensic legal study will not provide the wider understanding to be gained when the social context for the use of police powers is studied – the role of officer discretion and the socio-political and cultural factors that influence such discretion, for instance. Nor will the social consequences and implications of any given policing action, initiative or philosophy necessarily be fully understood without an appreciation both of the powers at police disposal and of the available alternatives to the use of such powers, particularly when crime detection (although a priority for politicians) represents a minority of the demands placed upon the police by the public.

In that vein, those undertaking police studies must adopt a multidisciplinary approach in order to achieve academic success. Policing is a skilled profession. No less professionalism is required of those who would study it.

1.2	
using this book	

Who should use this book? Students at any stage of their undergraduate or postgraduate careers in any of the disciplines already mentioned (or indeed others), who need a broad overview of any or all of the aspects of policing introduced here. Skim reading will provide a general introduction. Focusing on individual sections, particularly the features incorporated within the sections, will help the reader develop her or his understanding of that particular topic.

This general introductory volume is a supplement to the syllabuses and specialist textbooks that lecturers and tutors will recommend to their students. For the undergraduate, it can provide an initial overview and can then be used as a reference point or revision aid throughout the undergraduate career. For the postgraduate Masters student, it also provides a useful overview, while for the postgraduate researcher it may provide guidance to related topics and illustrate how and where other disciplines are engaged.

What this book will not do is give the reader *everything* he or she needs in order to pass assignments or exams. It is a study aid, not a substitute for study.

1.3

introducing the features

Being a successful student necessitates learning how to think and write theoretically and analytically. Key points and ideas must be identified, understood and clearly presented. There is an art to academic writing and discourse, and Part Three aims to help undergraduates develop core academic skills.

Successful assignments or exam essays will depend upon a sound answer construction to the question that is being posed. The difference between an adequate answer that will pass and a good answer that will attract extra marks will depend upon how widely read the student is, and how he or she develops the construction of their answer. The following features are employed in Part Two to provide sign-posts pointing the way from an adequate assignment or essay towards a good piece of work. They must, however, be used in conjunction with the *syllabus* and *learning outcomes* identified for the course of study being undertaken by the student. Best use of this volume will be made by those who understand what is expected of them by their lecturers.

Key thinkers/Key issues

Where appropriate 'key thinkers' (who may be practitioners or academics) or 'key issues', are identified and introduced and additional reference is made as required. This feature provides either a context within which to read the sub-section or the framework for the sub-section. Key thinkers and issues are likely to feature in answers and essays. For example:

Key thinkers

Sir David Phillips, John Grieve and **Brian Flood**, all senior police officers with considerable detective experience, pioneered intelligence-led policing in the 1990s. Their work was reinforced by two important reports: Audit Commission (1993) *Helping with Enquiries: Tackling Crime Effectively*, London: Audit Commission; and HMIC (1999) *Policing with Intelligence*, London: HMIC.

Case studies

Where used, these boxes give examples illustrating issues or key points.

Bullet point summaries

Where used, these boxes provide a checklist to summarise and highlight key points for students.

Taking it further

Probably the most frequently used feature, these boxed features pose questions for the reader to reflect upon when thinking about how to develop an answer to a particular topic. The questions posed could feature in an exam or as an assignment title. For example:

Taking it *FURTHER*

A useful area for further exploration is the relationship between public and private policing, especially in relation to the growing phenomenon of gated communities or in areas where local residents have hired their own private security. For instance, does the presence of private policing generate more work for the public police?

Tips

Boxed and signalled by a tack, Tips will help plan and structure answers, focusing on how to apply learning, how to analyse data and how to present a critical argument. For example:

> *There are two important areas to the study of criminal investigation, each linked to investigation quality. The first aspect is the legitimacy (including integrity) of investigation, the second concerns the practicalities of investigation management.*

Common pitfalls

Common mistakes and confusions lose marks. Where appropriate, these have been highlighted to assist the reader in avoiding such adverse consequences. For example:

> ***Common pitfalls:*** *Confusing the terms international and transnational policing in essays and exam answers will lose marks.*
>
> *Failing to acknowledge the key differences between different types of jurisdiction and legal tradition, which define domestic policing, will suggest to the examiner that the candidate does not fully appreciate the complexity of context within which transnational and international policing takes place.*

Textbook guide

Each section ends with a list of texts: either relevant laws, original/official documents or academic studies and secondary literature reviews that will broaden and develop the reader's understanding of the topic being presented. None of the lists is exhaustive but all supplement a broad introduction to the subject.

Additional resources

These are contained within Part Four. They comprise a glossary that includes abbreviations and useful websites, and a chronological table of laws and official documents relevant to the constitutional history of policing in England and Wales, which provides a framework with which to understand the developing organisation of policing. There is also a bibliography of additional reading, to supplement the key texts listed at the end of each section.

1.4

researching police organisations

This book is aimed at readers from a variety of disciplines at any stage of their student careers. Although in most undergraduate curricula research does not feature prominently until the third or fourth year of study and the production of a dissertation, it is never too early to use original/official source material in essays or assignments. Using such material will demonstrate to examiners an ability to identify and analyse data, thus illustrating that the student has developed beyond the mere recitation of secondary literature.

Much is available on the internet and official websites are listed in Part Four. Key sources of original information are the Home Office, the Association of Chief Police Officers (ACPO), Her Majesty's Inspector of Constabulary (HMIC), individual police forces, and various think tanks and civil liberties groups.

Individual organisations may not be in a position to respond to individual research requests but the Freedom of Information Act has resulted in a significant amount of material now being made available via the internet.

1.5

the study of policing: a brief introduction

Why police? Is it primarily to control crime or preserve the peace? This debate has accompanied policing since the foundation of the first public police forces in Britain in the late eighteenth and early nineteenth centuries. There is an eternal tension between these two core activities and they are sometimes mutually antagonistic and even exclusive. Theorists sometimes place one in the ascendancy, sometimes the other. Who benefits from policing and what are the benefits?

Who polices whom? It has been argued that the origins of policing lay in the desire of the property-owning socio-economic elite to keep under control those whose labour was required to produce the wealth controlled by so few. An alternative proposition is that policing can serve the interests of the state in subjugating a population. Increasingly, a number of activities traditionally undertaken by police forces are now being undertaken by other agencies or even private enterprise. Who decides what and who should be policed are questions which raise issues of governance and accountability. To what extent is it true that the British are policed by consent?

How is policing done? Thief-catching and preventative patrol have been at the core of policing since its earliest origins. Nowadays technology plays an increasing role and it could be argued that in some respects the population can at times be self-policing, even subconsciously. The ways in which people can be policed have expanded enormously, not least with the increased capability for covert investigation and surveillance. What tactics are permitted? What controls are in place?

When is policing done? Discretion lies at the heart of democratic policing and again raises issues of accountability. Which behaviours should be subject to policing? All drugs or just class A drugs? When are resources devoted to investigating crime and when does risk management dictate that crimes should go uninvestigated? How are these decisions made? By whom?

Where is policing done? Geographical jurisdiction introduces a myriad of permutations in police studies. At the national level there are some national police or police-like agencies but the UK has three different criminal jurisdictions (England and Wales, Scotland, and Northern Ireland) and each has different approaches to policing, not least because of different legal traditions and socio-political circumstances. A volume this size cannot hope to do justice, even in summary introduction, to these different domestic jurisdictions, so the focus here will be on general aspects of policing and, in relation to police powers, the law of England and Wales, purely on the basis that this encompasses the majority of the British population.

What are the problems posed by policing? Since policing involves the use of coercion in a variety of forms (arrest, search, the acquisition by the state of an individual's biometric data) there immediately arise issues of legitimacy, proportionality, necessity, transparency and oversight. How are these resolved? When the police get it wrong, what redress exists for individuals or society as a whole? And with an increasing amount of public space now policed by non-police entities, how are the rights of citizens protected against abuse by police and non-police actors?

This brief introduction has served to illustrate the complexity of policing and so the complexity of studying policing. The reader will no doubt already have thought of other *why, who, how, when, where* and *what* questions that could just have easily been used to illustrate the point of this introduction. That is both the breadth and fascination of police studies.

Answering these questions could take a lifetime of study, not least because as society develops and changes so the expectations of and needs for policing change. There are no easy solutions and rarely a simple choice between the right and wrong answers. Approaches to answering these questions form the content of Part Two, the curriculum section of this book.

Part Two is divided into three over-arching themes within which a number of sub-sections are presented. The intention is to draw the reader's attention to the wide variety of possible subject areas within policing as well as highlighting areas of interrelationship. Part Two commences with subjects that comprise the overall framework of policing provision, including structures, governance, public engagement and police reform. The second theme focuses on the practice of policing from a strategic perspective, highlighting wider implications in preference to merely describing how policing is done. The third theme examines the cultural contexts, at both organisational and wider society levels, within which policing takes place. Part Three presents guidance to undergraduates on core academic skills and how these can be applied in police studies. Part Four either provides or points the reader towards additional resources, such as a glossary of terms and acronyms (including relevant useful websites), a chronological table of key laws and policy documents relating to the constitution of policing in England and Wales, and a select bibliography of texts cited in the book and additional reading, arranged thematically by section.

part two
policing

running themes in policing

Other volumes in the Course Companions series illustrate running themes that students should at least consider, if not include, when answering any exam question or researching any course assignment. Hence Ursula Smartt identified human rights, inequality, fear of crime, victims, race, gender, punishment, globalisation, criminalisation, and crime and the media as running themes when considering criminal justice as an abstract area of study (Smartt, *Criminal Justice*, Sage, 2006).

While it is equally possible to consider the above as abstract concepts when studying policing, policing is also a socio-political reality as well as a sub-discipline within academic criminology. Policing happens every day to real people. Police officers often have only seconds or a few minutes to consider and act upon issues that students, researchers and lawyers have years to study.

Hence issues such as gender, race and human rights warrant sections in their own right in this volume. The running themes to consider when studying policing should perhaps be better described as running perspectives. Thus any given section may (and should) be viewed from the varying perspectives of the **police organisation, staff** within a police organisation, **victims, suspects**, third parties such as **witnesses, other agencies** and the **wider community**, and from different **political perspectives**. Unless the question posed requires that all these different perspectives be considered in relation to a given theme, it may not be appropriate (or even feasible) to include a considered discussion of each perspective in an answer or assignment. But students should recognise that any permutation of these perspectives, if not all of them, can apply to any given theme and, if necessary, should explain why academic constraints have obliged a student to focus only on certain perspectives and not others.

The recruitment, retention and career progression of ethnic minority officers, for instance, is a race issue within policing which might be considered from any or all of the perspectives of the ethnic officers, the organisation and the community being policed.

It is equally possible that a question on policing ethnic minorities may require consideration from the perspectives of ethnic minority victims, or ethnic minority suspects, or ethnic minority officers (as both individuals and representatives of the police) policing an ethnic majority community (and in some urban areas a white community beat police officer might be an ethnic minority of one), or ethnic majority officers (as both individuals and representatives of the police) policing an ethnic minority community. The latter, of course, is a perspective often examined in relation to the Brixton riots, stop and search and the Macpherson Report. But it is not the only perspective.

Balancing conflicting human rights is another multifaceted arena in which the rights of suspect, victim, wider community and police staff may conflict and for which more than one perspective exists.

The use to which **statistics** and **sources** are put to inform any of the identified perspectives is a further running theme that students should consider. On what basis is any given government policy or policing strategy devised? How informed really are the politicians? The police? The public? From where are perceptions and perspectives derived? Evidenced-based policy-making and knowledge-based policing are areas of ongoing academic research.

Studying policing methodologically is little different from policing itself. The key questions are always who, what, where, when, how and why? Above all, why?

the policing framework	

2.1	
the emergence and history of policing	

Core areas: **Emergence of professional 'police' in the eighteenth century**
Increasing demand for public policing
Consolidation of policing

Although 'policing' – the maintenance of law and order – is documented from the early Middle Ages, professional policing (and its associated recurring dichotomies: crime detection or peace preservation; local or central control) did not emerge until the eighteenth century. Later sections introduce twentieth-century developments (Sections 2.3 to 2.6). This section identifies relevant developments up to the present day and should be read in conjunction with Section 4.2 detailing the constitutional history of English policing.

Running themes

It is instructive to reflect upon how **victim**, **wider community** and **third-party** perspectives of crime and disorder have influenced the development of **police organisations** and the expectations imposed on **police officers and staff**. How has the **use of statistics**, for instance, influenced **political perspectives** and **policy-making**? Policing today is the outcome of an evolution in which the above running themes played an important role. But has it resulted in what is needed for the twenty-first century?

Emergence of professional 'police' in the eighteenth century

Eighteenth-century socio-economic developments (increasing industrialisation and urbanisation) necessitated development in the law and its application. Innovations in trial procedure (active participation of lawyers) and punishment (transportation) were matched with new ideas about policing.

Hitherto it was the victim's responsibility to investigate crime, gather evidence and initiate proceedings. To service this need, professional thief-takers, who were paid a fee upon successful convictions, undertook private criminal investigations. Corruption was common; regulation, non-existent.

In 1750, novelist and magistrate, Henry Fielding, formed the first professional body of investigators, operating from his magistrates office in Bow Street, thus establishing embryonic concepts of professional police and policing. In 1792 this group of investigators was given a statutory basis under the Middlesex Justice Act and became known as the *Bow Street Runners*, thus establishing the concepts of professional police and policing. 'What was new was their systematic publicising of the notion that social control was attainable – and worth attaining through an organised institutional effort' (Rawlings 1996, p. 143). Henry Fielding believed that social control would be achieved by introducing a proactive system of crime detection that would be directed by a state bureaucracy working under the Justices of the Peace and also by the rigorous regulation of the poor.

Originally eight in number, within two years there were 80 Runners. Similar to the unofficial 'thief-takers', they represented a formalisation and regularisation of existing policing methods. What distinguished them was their formal attachment to the Bow Street Magistrates office, being paid by the magistrate with funds from central government. They served writs and arrested offenders on the authority of the magistrates but did not patrol the streets.

Although the force was only funded intermittently in the years that followed, it did serve as the guiding principal for the way policing was to develop over the next 80 years. They were disbanded in 1839.

Increasing demand for public policing

The Gordon Riots (1780) exposed government inability to deal with major public disorder. During the riots much of London succumbed to anarchy and in the aftermath there were many calls to introduce a police 'force' to prevent further disturbances. Prime Minister William Pitt unsuccessfully sought to establish a body of full-time peace-keepers (London and Westminster Police Bill 1785). Parliament feared the repressive style system of policing prevailing in revolutionary France. Nevertheless, the notion of a full-time police was gaining popularity.

A decade later, Patrick Colquhoun, a magistrate, considered the potential for a full-time police in his *Treatise on the Policing of the Metropolis* (1797). He argued that the benefits of having a full-time police, particularly in the dock area of London, would greatly outweigh the costs in terms of the prevention of the theft of cargo.

Colquhoun's *Treatise* led to the creation of the *Thames River Police* in 1800. The sole objective of the first police force so-called was the prevention and detection of crime in the Thames dockyards. It was absorbed into London's Metropolitan Police in 1839.

The increasing influence of the Home Office in policing gained momentum when Sir Robert Peel became Home Secretary in 1820. He determined to reform the criminal justice system in England. As Chief Secretary for Ireland (1812–18), he had established the Royal Irish

Constabulary. This provided the impetus for his unsuccessful campaign for a national English police force but the excesses of the military yeomanry during the Peterloo massacre (1819), and continued concerns about the roles undertaken by continental police forces, undermined support for such a force.

For Peel's Nine Principles of Policing see section 2.5 below.

While Peel's attempt to introduce a national police force failed, he did establish the *Metropolitan Police* in 1829. Peel shrewdly circumvented opposition from the independent-minded Aldermen of the City of London by excluding the 'square mile' jurisdiction from the Bill. The first Metropolitan Police Constables patrolled the streets of London in September 1829. (The City of London introduced its own police force in 1839).

From its inception the Metropolitan Police was seen as a means to establish and maintain a new threshold of law and order. The first two Metropolitan Police Commissioners, Colonel Charles Rowan and Richard Mayne (a lawyer), ensured that although the new organisation was hierarchical, disciplined and regimented, it was not a military institution.

Consolidation of policing

The next century, up until the post-Second World War period, witnessed the consolidation of policing along two themes: the *provision of policing* and the *professionalism* of the service. The constitutional chronology is detailed in Section 4.2 below.

The widespread provision of professional policing began in towns (once initial concerns about how the Metropolitan Police was developing had waned). Criminals soon learnt to evade urban police by escaping to the un-policed rural hinterlands, thus creating a demand for rural policing. Local authorities, such as they were in the second half of the nineteenth century, were anxious to avoid having policing provided by central government.

Professionalism in policing varied extensively despite the creation of an Inspectorate – Her Majesty's Inspectorate of Constabulary (HMIC) – to ensure standards (1856). By 1900 there were over 250 forces widely diverse in size, skills and training. Few had specialist detectives, and pay and conditions were generally poor. Following the First World War, a committee chaired by Lord Desborough reviewed police pay and service conditions, laying the foundation for practices that prevailed until the New Public Management era of the 1980s.

In the 1950s significant increases in crime prompted the first full-scale consideration of what policing was needed, and how it might best be provided, since Peel's nine principles of 1829. The outcome was the Royal Commission on Policing, 1960–62. Changes in criminality, increased interaction between different communities and a more mobile population militated against the tenets of local law and order. The Royal Commission on Policing, together with another Royal Commission on Local Government, accelerated a process of force amalgamations that had been taking place ever since the creation of professional forces. The issues that local policing was being asked to address were becoming increasingly non-local. But despite a strong dissenting opinion within the Royal Commission on Policing that the time had come for a national police force, the principle of local policing, locally controlled, was reiterated within the concept of the tripartite relationship (see Section 2.3)

Law and order assumed a different national political prominence in the 1979 general election. Hitherto political parties had not made policing an election issue but now the Conservative party specifically attacked the Labour government's law and order record. Under Margaret Thatcher's premiership, the drive for enhanced performance management was a further permutation that added to the tensions between local and national policing provision, and debates about the exact functions a public police service should perform. Subsequent sections discuss these issues in more detail.

The period of policing consolidation was over. Now the debate focuses on what policing is needed in the twenty-first century and how its provision should move from the Victorian infrastructure preserved by the 1960 Royal Commission, to a service that is 'fit for purpose' in the modern era.

"Identify and define the key developments in nineteenth-century English policing."

Part Four provides a chronological framework of legislative developments from which a student might select key Acts that determine significant developments.

Alternatively, a thematic approach might be adopted, perhaps focusing on the functional tensions between peace preservation and crime investigation.

Taking it *FURTHER*

Those wishing to learn more about pre-modern 'policing' must turn to historical rather than criminological studies.

Beattie J (2001) *Policing and Punishment in London 1660–1750*, Oxford: Oxford University Press
Bellamy J (1973) *Crime and Public Order in England in the Later Middle Ages*, London: Routledge
McKisack M (1959) *The Fourteenth Century 1307–1399*, Oxford: Clarendon Press (Chapter 7)
Morris W (1927) *The Medieval English Sheriff*, Manchester: Manchester University Press
Poole A (1955) *From Domesday Book to Magna Carta* (2nd edn), Oxford: Clarendon Press (Chapter 12)

Textbook guide

CRITCHLEY T (1978) *A History of the Police in England and Wales*, London: Constable
EMSLEY C (1996) *The English Police: A Political and Social History* (2nd edn), London: Longman
NEWBURN T (ED.) (2005) *Policing: Key Readings*, Cullompton: Willan (Part A)
RAWLINGS P (2002) *Policing: A Short History*, Cullompton: Willan

2.2

the function and role of the police

Core areas: **The primary functions**

Peace-keepers or crime fighters?

The specialisation and pluralisation of policing

Policing permeates and impacts upon all aspects of society. In the UK policing purports to be 'by consent' rather than a state-directed military model. Thus its success is dependent on public co-operation and approval rather than fear. The police are called upon routinely to perform a wide range of tasks from public reassurance to terrorism. One of the uniting features of police work is that they respond to emergencies, critical incidents and crises, many with an element of social conflict. However, understanding the function and role of the police requires consideration of the philosophy and ideology of policing. This assumes greater significance in the context of the legitimate authority, monopolisation of force and social control aspect of policing.

Running themes

What the police do or should be doing is influenced by a variety of perspectives: those of **police organisations, police officers and staff, victims, third parties** and **other agencies** and the **wider community**. The **use of statistics** will inform **political perspectives** and **policy-making**.

The primary functions

If Sir Robert Peel's principles still hold true today, then the original tenets of policing have not changed. This would imply that the primary function of the police is upholding the Queen's law and maintaining peace through:

- the prevention of crime
- detection of offenders if crime is committed
- protection of life and property
- the preservation of public tranquillity

Thus the role of the police can be defined by a set of activities and processes with a broad mandate to prevent, detect and control crime and disorder.

> Jones & Newburn (1998, pp. 18–19) define policing as: 'those organised forms of order-maintenance, peacekeeping, rule or law enforcement and other forms of investigation and information-brokering – which may involve a conscious exercise of coercive power – undertaken by individuals or organisations, where such activities are viewed by them and/or others as a central defining part of their purpose.'

Understanding the complex and multidimensional function of policing requires consideration of the following:

Legal	These are the state powers conferred on the police in order for them legitimately to fulfil their operational duties, including the use of force to uphold the law
Sectoral	This describes the relationships between the police and other non-governmental policing organisations. This is becoming more complex as security issues are becoming increasingly privatised
Geographical	Different police organisations are responsible for different geographical locations, including local, national and international areas
Spatial	Control and policing of different spaces, such as residential, industrial, commercial, governmental, cyberspace
Information brokers	Collation, analysis, and dissemination of information/ intelligence. Used for directing, as well as the risk assessment and management of, policing activities

Peace-keepers or crime fighters?

Crime fighting and the maintenance or keeping of the peace are two distinctive styles of policing. Although significantly different, they are not necessarily mutually exclusive. Crime fighting is the active pursuit or response to current and immediate criminal activity, whereas keeping the peace seeks to ensure that these activities do not occur in the first place through obvious police presence, community policing and effective community relations, allowing the police to circumvent or prevent crime before it occurs. The model favoured at any particular time depends upon political preference, tensions within communities, and socio-economic determinants.

Crime fighting is characterised by strong, centralised command and control with limited contact with the public. It is premised on a para-military model that emphasises 'crime fighting' and order maintenance rather than crime prevention. The police are generally equipped with an array of protective clothes and crime-fighting tools, such as truncheons and CS gas. Thus the police become a highly visible symbolic image representing the state. The police will normally invoke their legal powers as crime fighters.

However, in their day-to-day tasks, the police normally operate in a peace-keeping role (see section 2.9 below). This is characterised by the police resolving problems through the use of discretion and negotiation. The situation is managed informally and legal proceedings or official action are not usually initiated. The police engage closely with the communities they police and work proactively by adopting a problem-oriented policing stance. Thus policing is more proactive than reactive. The image associated with peace-keeping is that of 'Dixon of Dock Green', with the community knowing the local beat officer. This approach has been endorsed through neighbourhood policing with greater devolution of responsibility to local commanders who provide a dedicated team of police officers and community support officers for specific areas.

The specialisation and pluralisation of policing

The fear of crime has become a dominant feature of society, coinciding with the apparent inability of the police to tackle increasing rates of recorded crime and disorder by themselves (Garland 2001). This has three significant consequences: first, the reorganisation of the division of labour within the police and the growth of specialist departments; secondly, the need for police to work closely with other agencies and organisations in partnership; and thirdly, the rise in private policing provision such as security companies. However, despite the escalation of private security companies the police still retain primacy in responding to emergencies and crises.

The nature and extent of plural policing can be illustrated with some examples (see the table below).

This table demonstrates that the police are not the monopolistic provider of policing functions. Rather, policing is delivered by a complex and ambiguous network of agents and organisations, some undertaking the activities of the police while others underwrite policing functions. The specialisation of crime control has led to a proliferation of providers and the development of security networks. In addition, there has been a shift from the state providing security to greater citizen involvement and responsibility. At the same time the structure and arrangement of police forces are changing with a parallel emphasis on

Specialist policing departments:	Providers of specialist services/assistance:
• Domestic Violence Unit • Criminal Investigation Department • Child Abuse Investigation Unit • Economic Crime Unit • Firearms Unit • Tactical Support Unit • Underwater and Search Department	• Serious and Organised Crime Agency • HM Customs and Revenue • Crime and Disorder Partnerships • Non-Home Office Forces • MI5 • MI6
Private policing organisations:	Civilian policing
• Security Guards • Private Detective Agencies • Door Supervisors • Private CCTV Equipment	• Special Constables • Neighbourhood Watch • Police Volunteers • Crimewatch
Municipal policing and regulation:	Partnership policing:
• Environmental Health Officers • Traffic Wardens • Anti-social Behaviour Teams • Trading Standards Officers • Health and Safety Officers	• Crime and Disorder Partnerships • Housing Associations • Youth Offending Teams • Drug Action Teams

both local delivery through Basic or Borough Command Units (BCU) and the restructuring of the service by the greater amalgamation of forces.

❝ Given the increased pluralisation of policing provision, what are the defining elements of a public police service? ❞

Answers are likely to include reference to state responsibilities for law and order; exclusive agency access to legitimate coercion and the use of force; and universal public access to state assistance in crime crises.

Taking it *FURTHER*

What influence has New Public Management and the increased focus on performance management had on the definition of 'policing'? See Neyroud P (2003), 'Policing and ethics', in Newburn T (ed.), *Handbook of Policing*, Cullompton: Willan, pp. 578–602, for a useful overview of recent changing philosophies/definitions of policing.

Textbook guide

FINDLEY M & ZUEKIV U (EDS) **(1993)** *Alternative Policing Styles: Cross-cultural Perspectives, Boston: Kluwer.*

JONES T & NEWBURN T **(1997)** *Policing after the Act: Police Governance after the Police and Magistrates Court Act, London: Policy Studies Institute*

NEWBURN T (ED.) **(2003)** *Handbook of Policing, Cullompton: Willan*

NEWBURN T (ED.) **(2005)** *Policing: Key Readings, Cullompton: Willan*

2.3
governance, structure and accountability

Core areas: **Local and national**
Tripartite arrangement
The three Es and managerialism
Her Majesty's Inspectorate of Constabulary (HMIC)
The Independent Police Complaints Commission (IPCC)
The National Policing Improvement Agency (NPIA)
The Association of Chief Police Officers (ACPO) and leadership

Running themes

These issues can be characterised by different, sometimes conflicting perspectives. **Police organisations**, **police officers and staff** may well have very different views on governance and accountability from **victims, suspects, third parties** and **other agencies**. The **wider community** will demonstrate a kaleidoscope of perspectives influenced by any or all of socio-economic context, ethnicity, religion, gender, and sexual orientation. As views are articulated into **political positions**, **statistics** may be invoked to support calls for greater accountability and stronger governance.

Local and national

The police in England and Wales do not operate as one centralised organisational entity. Rather, the police service comprises 43 separate organisations that are responsible for policing local territory. However, with the exception of the City of London, all forces have been subject to amalgamations and boundary changes. Each force has developed its own distinctive character, informed by historical and geographical demands. Collaborative arrangements are common in relation to a number of policing activities, such as asset recovery, motorway patrol and helicopter support. Allowing for some local variation, each force has a similar organisational infrastructure. Each force has a headquarters that accommodates the management team, and specialist and support departments. The geographical area of the force is divided into Basic Command Units (BCUs) that are responsible for delivering local policing. BCU boundaries are generally coterminous with local authority boundaries to assist in statutory partnership working and co-operation.

Although British policing remains embedded as a decentralised local arrangement, it has been recognised that this structure is not suitable for all forms of crime. Specialist crimes, such as terrorism and drug trafficking, which require dedicated support functions, need a different response, as does crime that is committed nationally or internationally. This capability gap has been articulated by the Home Office (2004) and HMIC (2005), and, to a limited extent, addressed by the creation of the Serious Organised Crime Agency (SOCA), an innovation which has brought its own challenges of governance and accountability (Harfield 2006). In contrast to neighbourhood policing these non-local issues have been termed 'protective services'.

Tripartite arrangement

The 1964 Police Act was integral in formalising the traditional architecture of policing, dividing responsibility between the Home Secretary, local police authorities and chief constables. The Home Secretary has the overall responsibility for the police service in terms of policy. The operational 'direction and control' of each force falls to the chief constables, with the police authorities overseeing their work to ensure an 'efficient and effective' police service for their area (s. 6, Police Act 1996).

This three-way system theoretically minimises central government interference in policing, ensuring that no single organisation dominates the activities or functions of the police force. In reality, the Home Office is the dominant partner.

In Scotland, the Justice Minister has responsibility for the eight police forces. The Northern Ireland Office oversees policing in the province.

Police authorities maintain each force in England and Wales, and pursuant to the Police and Magistrates Courts Act 1994 (as consolidated in the Police Act 1996), they comprise local councillors, magistrates and independent members. Each authority receives central government grants and appoints a chief constable to their region, subject to the approval of the Home Secretary. Until the creation of the Metropolitan Police Authority in 1999, the Metropolitan Police Service (MPS) was accountable directly to the Home Secretary.

The three Es and managerialism

The Thatcher administration sought reform of the public sector through the philosophy of New Public Management (NPM). For the police service, this first found expression in promotion of the three Es – economy, efficiency and effectiveness – in Home Office Circular 114/83. This was reinforced with a series of research papers from the Audit Commission during the late 1980s and early 1990s.

Of particular emphasis in NPM were monetary restraints and the need to provide a 'value for money' service to the community. In addition, the government diverted attention away from finding the causes of crime towards the measurement of crime and the efficacy of the police service. The concept of policing by performance objectives was now routinely applied and inspected.

Her Majesty's Inspectorate of Constabulary (HMIC)

Her Majesty's Inspectors (HMIs) of Constabulary are charged with examining and improving the efficiency of the Police Service in England and Wales (and latterly Northern Ireland), with the first HMIs appointed under the provisions of the County and Borough Police Act 1856. The HMIC ensures that the policing standards are universally met, promotes efficiency and effectiveness and ensures that:

- agreed standards are achieved and maintained
- good practice is spread
- performance is improved.

HMIC inspectors have independent status and conduct regular inspections on all forces, including BCUs. They undertake thematic inspections and 'best value' inspections, the latter giving the HMIC effective oversight of police authorities, which have a statutory responsibility for ensuring 'best value'.

The Independent Police Complaints Commission (IPCC)

The Independent Police Complaints Commission (IPCC) is the organisation that has overall responsibility for the system of complaints against the police. It was formed in 2004, replacing the Police Complaints Authority. The IPCC functions to secure and keep under review the maintenance of suitable arrangements for the recording, handling and investigation of complaints and conduct matters and operates with an appropriate degree of independence. The IPCC is competent to make reports and recommendations to the Home Secretary on police practices. Its investigators have full police powers while on duty (although at the time of writing these had never yet been used) and must by law be given access to police premises, documents and other evidence when requested.

The National Policing Improvement Agency (NPIA)

While not formally part of police accountability mechanisms, the National Policing Improvement Agency (NPIA) is a new body that that will become operational in 2007 and its primary function will be to support forces and improve the way they work across many areas of policing. The NPIA will replace the existing national policing organisations such as the Police Information Technology Organisation (PITO) and Centrex, and take on some new work needed to support national policing improvement.

One of the agency's key roles will be to support the local implementation of the government's 'mission critical' policing priorities, detailed in the National Community Safety Plan (which replaces the National Policing Plan introduced by the Police Reform Act 2002). These include implementation of the Bichard Inquiry recommendations, Neighbourhood Policing and Level 2 Crime. The NPIA will review current practice, challenge how it is being done and establish what improvements can be made. The NPIA will provide a number of benefits, including the improved co-ordination of major national projects that were previously managed by separate organisations.

The Association of Chief Police Officers (ACPO) and leadership

The Association of Chief Police Officers (ACPO) is an independent, professionally led strategic body, established in 1948, with the aim of centralising the development of policing strategies within one body, on behalf of the service as a whole rather than by separate forces. The ACPO comprises officers of the rank of assistant chief constables and above and police staff equivalent. The collective strength of ACPO has grown into a substantial lobbying and policy-making body. ACPO promotes leadership excellence and provides strategic headship both locally and nationally. One of the biggest challenges facing ACPO in the twenty-first century is to develop police forces, in conjunction with NPIA development of practice, that can effectively recognise, relate and respond to shifts in criminal activity, changing communities and their expectations, workforce modernisation, technology, the political agenda, policing philosophies and legislative constraints.

❝What are the different contributions of police authorities and the HMIC in influencing policing priorities?❞

This invites a compare/contrast approach which could start by outlining the different statutory remits. The extent to which HMIC inspections and reviews influence Home Office priorities and the National Policing Plan/National Community Safety Plan, within whose constraints police authorities draft their local policing plans, could usefully be discussed.

 Taking it **FURTHER**

An issue on which there is a sizeable literature is the extent to which the balance of power in the supposedly equal tripartite relationship is in fact asymmetrical. The evolution of this relationship since 1964 is still much debated.

Textbook guide

JONES T & NEWBURN T (1993) *Policing After the Act: Police Governance after the Police and Magistrates Act 1994, London: Policy Studies Institute*
NEWBURN T (ED.) (2003) *Handbook of Policing, Cullompton: Willan, especially Chapters 23–25*
WALKER N (2000) *Policing in a Changing Constitutional Order, London: Sweet & Maxwell*

2.4
public engagement and the police

Running themes

The need for succinct section headings should not confuse the reader. This section needs to be read within the context of public engagement with the police and police engagement with the public. **Police organisations**, **police officers and staff** may well have very different views on the purpose of and appropriate mechanisms for engagement from **victims**, **suspects**, **third parties** and **other agencies**. The **wider community** will demonstrate a kaleidoscope of perspectives influenced by any or all of socio-economic context, ethnicity, religion, gender, and sexual orientation. As views are articulated into **political positions**, **statistics** may be invoked to support calls for greater accountability and stronger governance.

Key issue

British policing has traditionally been founded on policing by consent. But how informed is that consent? And how is it obtained?

Constitutional relationship

Sir Robert Peel asserted (1829) that the police should seek and preserve public favour *not by catering to public opinion* but by constantly demonstrating absolute impartial service to the law (see Section 2.5 below). The Desborough Committee (1918–19, Section 4.2) noted that constables act not as agents of government but as citizens representing and working on behalf of 'the community', *to whom the police owe a sense of obligation.* Prime Minister Tony Blair's philosophy seeks to implement *citizen-focused* public services, involving the community in arriving at solutions. The 1980s and 1990s witnessed a widespread desire to hold the police more accountable, not just at court for individual investigations, but also to government for resource expenditure and to the community for strategies and general performance.

Modes of engagement

The public engage with the police in two ways: as individual citizens and as 'communities'. The police engage with the public as investigators, peace-keepers, law enforcers and service providers.

By September 2005 there were 143,000 UK police officers, a national citizen–police ratio of approximately 420:1 (subject to geographic variation). The British Crime Survey 2004/05 found that 40% of adults had had some contact with the police in the previous year, fewer than in recent years. Twenty-two per cent experienced police-initiated contact (82% of whom were satisfied with police handling of the contact), while 28% initiated their own contact (65% of whom were satisfied with police-handling of the contact). Paradoxically, the same survey found that overall confidence in the police generally decreased after actual contact with the police. Nevertheless, a number of Mori polls appear to indicate that the majority of the public (59%) trust police officers (even if there is an increasing dissatisfaction with the standards of policing – which is seen as a government issue, not a police issue), and that the police are more widely trusted than civil servants (45%), government ministers (20%) or journalists (13%).

Common pitfall: *Question structure influences survey responses. Students must be careful, when using such data, to ensure that the use to which the data is put relates to the survey questions that were asked.*

Surveys routinely demonstrate a public desire to see more police foot patrols, regardless of the fact that this is the most inefficient use of resources when trying to respond to all the specific, incident-based demands made by the public of the police. Individual, citizen-initiated contact with the police is generally technological rather than interpersonal, that is by telephone and the internet. The volume of calls made to the police has risen exponentially in recent decades, partly through increased public access to telephones. Where once a traffic accident, for example, might be reported by a single individual using a nearby telephone kiosk, now the same incident may be reported by a significant number of individuals using mobile phones. For the police this has the benefit of enhanced witness identification but creates a problem in volume call-handling that has to be managed.

Such are the individual demands placed on the police that call management, including strategies of delayed response by appointment to non-urgent incidents or taking reports of minor crime by telephone/ internet only, has become a key area of work for police managers.

POLICE–PUBLIC INTERACTION PERSPECTIVES

- Victims
- Witnesses
- Offenders
- Ethnic minorities
- Gender
- Generation
- Consumers of media dramas or 'fly-on-the-wall' documentaries

How might these perspectives influence perceptions of an encounter with the police?

TYPES OF INTERACTION

- Personal encounter with a patrolling officer
- Telephone contact initiated by a citizen
- Visit to police station
- Internet
- Police-initiated contact (stop and search, vehicle stop, witness-seeking)
- Consultation groups
- Satisfaction surveys/opinion polls

Influencing the police agenda

If citizen incident-based demand drives much of a police officer's daily work, how can communities influence longer-term policing strategies? Peel maintained that the police should not be swayed by public opinion – a majority opinion might give rise to oppressive policing of a minority – but government now requires citizen-focused service delivery and community-led solutions. How can this circle be squared?

CASE STUDY

In the 1990s one urban police sub-division comprised eight square miles encompassing both impoverished inner-city areas and affluent suburbs. Its resident population of 40,000 swelled to 60,000 during university terms. Its daily population vastly exceeded the resident population due to workers commuting into the city. All the major religions were represented, including several Christian denominations. Minority communities from across the world (but particularly from the Indian sub-continent, the Caribbean, the Middle East and the Orient) lived within the sub-division and ethnicity-based conflict overseas occasionally ignited sub-divisional inter-community tensions. In addition to the permanently settled population there were a number of homeless people who resided on the streets and travellers who were temporarily but regularly resident from time to time. It also hosted a sizeable vice area and drugs market, both of which serviced an area geographically far bigger than the sub-division. All of these are communities.

Police restructuring into BCUs merged this cosmopolitan and complex sub-division with two neighbouring sub-divisions, each of which had their own equally complex community profiles. Community relations permutations were magnified with the merger and at the Force-level perspective.

Communities can be defined by, for example, ethnicity, employment, territory, gender, sexual orientation, religion, age, lifestyle. The only common feature of these disparate yet neighbouring and inter-mingling case study communities was their co-location within an artificial territorial boundary delimiting the command responsibilities of the local police superintendent. The only certainty arising from this melting pot of perspectives was that there would be no consensus on how the community should be policed.

Police authorities have statutory obligations to consult the public when determining local policing strategies. Consultation can take place in a variety of ways but will almost always include community meetings and satisfaction surveys. Home Office research in 2003 established that a large majority of the public remain ignorant about police authorities, begging questions about how effectively authorities engage with the public. The effectiveness of police community consultation groups, recommended by Lord Scarman after his inquiry into the Brixton riots, has been much studied and questioned.

How knowledgeable are the public generally about policing problems and potential solutions? The identified need for a National Reassurance Policing Programme seeks primarily to address public perceptions and fears of rising crime which prevail despite the reality that crime is falling. To what extent can a public that lacks awareness of police powers and capability, and the problems as they really exist, contribute meaningfully to community-based policing solutions and to strategic debate? The pages of *Hansard* reveal to the specialist that MPs often display only a rudimentary layperson's (mis)understanding of policing issues. If MPs, supported by parliamentary researchers and in constant touch with their constituents, remain insufficiently aware of the issues, what can reasonably be expected from the public?

The extent to which community priorities can be incorporated into local policing plans is further constrained by the need for the police to comply with national priorities and performance targets dictated by the Home Office.

"Who sets the local policing agenda?"

One possible approach to answering this question would be to demonstrate an understanding of how the national policing performance framework is established and measured; how local policing plans are established; the relationship between these two; how and if local communities are consulted about policing priorities; and which of the various sources informing a local policing agenda has primacy.

"Policing by consent is a myth. Discuss."

If citizens have to obey the law, what does policing by consent actually mean? How are the views/consent of the community obtained when determining what and how to police? In a cosmopolitan society with any given police area comprising any number of 'communities' defined by a variety of geographic, socio-economic, ethnic and religious criteria, is consent – or even consensus – really achievable? If society is not policed by consent, how is it policed?

Taking it *FURTHER*

Police authorities have a statutory duty to maintain 'an efficient and effective police force' for their areas (s. 6 Police Act 1996). They also have a duty to consult the public about policing (s. 96). How effective are police authorities in executing the duty to engage with and consult the public? Reference to official reports as well as secondary literature will widen understanding of this issue.

Harfield C (1997) 'Whose plan is it anyway? Consent, consensus and the management of dissent: challenges to community consultation in a new policing environment', *Policing & Society* 7, pp. 271–289

Home Office (2003) *The Role of Police Authorities in Public Engagement*, London: Home Office Online Report 37/03

Home Office (2006) *Policing and the Criminal Justice System – Public Confidence and Perceptions: Findings from the 2004/05 British Crime Survey*, London: Home Office Online Report 07/06

Home Office Research, Development & Statistics Directorate (2006) *An Evaluation of the Impact of the National Reassurance Policing Programme*, London: Home Office

Textbook guide

CRAWFORD A & GOODEY J (EDS) (2000) *Integrating a Victim Perspective within Criminal Justice, Aldershot: Ashgate*

JONES T (2003) *'The governance and accountability of policing', in T Newburn (ed.), Handbook of Policing, Cullompton: Willan, pp. 603–627.*

LONG M (2003) *'Leadership and performance management', in T Newburn (ed.), Handbook of Policing, Cullompton: Willan, pp. 628–54.*

SAVAGE S ET AL. (2000) *'The policy-making in context: who shapes policing policy?', in F Leishman et al. (eds), Core Issues in Policing, Harlow: Longman, pp. 30–51*

2.5

philosophies of policing – keeping the peace and enforcing the law

Core areas: **Peel's principles of policing**

Problem-oriented policing

Zero tolerance policing

Total geographic policing

Intelligence-led policing

Neighbourhood policing

Risk management policing

There are many different views on what policing is for and how it should be undertaken. This section introduces the key philosophies that have dominated practical, academic and political thinking about policing. Should the focus of policing be on tackling crime or the causes of crime? How should the police connect with the community? How can finite resources best be deployed? Should the police have to do all the policing? All these questions have given rise to different philosophies of policing.

Running themes

How might any or each of the following influence interpretation of this topic? Will the corporate views of **police organisations** differ from those of individual **police officers and staff**? Will different perspectives on justice (restitution or retribution; rights protection for the accused) incline **victims**, **third parties**, **the wider community** and **suspects** to either one philosophical approach or another? What might be the different consequences for **third parties** and **other agencies** of any one particular philosophy? And if different **political perspectives** favour different policing philosophies, what **statistical data** exist to enable an objective and impartial observer to evaluate the different approaches?

> *Common pitfall:* When required to compare/contrast two different philosophies, avoid the trap of analysing one but only describing the other and ensure that both similarities and differences are discussed.

Key thinkers

Sir Robert Peel (1829) institutionalised the concept of preventative patrol.

Herman Goldstein (1979) established problem-oriented policing as a structured alternative to random patrolling.

James Wilson and **George Kelling** (1982) argued that zero tolerance towards 'broken windows' would prevent crime escalation and urban degeneration.

Ericson and **Haggerty** (1997) proposed a risk management approach to policing

Sir David Phillips, **John Grieve** and **Brian Flood** between them developed and contributed to the concept of the intelligence-led policing in the UK during the 1990s.

The **Home Office** has supported total geographic policing (Brownlee and Walker, 1998), and now promotes a Neighbourhood Policing/reassurance agenda (2004).

Peel's principles of policing

Peel's founding principles for the Metropolitan Police (1829) defined, for over 100 years, preventative patrol as the key to successful policing. Victorian constables had set patrol routes (beats) that took ten minutes to patrol. Any citizen needing the police, in theory, could stand on a main street or junction and within ten minutes a police officer would pass by.

PEEL'S NINE PRINCIPLES OF POLICING

1. The basic mission for which the police exist is to prevent crime and disorder.
2. The ability of the police to perform their duties is dependent upon public approval of police actions.
3. Police must secure the willing co-operation of the public in voluntary observance of the law to be able to secure and maintain the respect of the public.
4. The degree of co-operation of the public that can be secured diminishes proportionately to the necessity of the use of physical force.

(Continued)

5. Police seek and preserve public favour not by catering to public opinion but by constantly demonstrating absolute impartial service to the law.
6. Police use physical force to the extent necessary to secure observance of the law or to restore order only when the exercise of persuasion, advice and warning is found to be insufficient.
7. Police, at all times, should maintain a relationship with the public that gives reality to the historic tradition that the police are the public and the public are the police; the police being only members of the public who are paid to give full-time attention to duties which are incumbent on every citizen in the interests of community welfare and existence.
8. Police should always direct their action strictly towards their functions and never appear to usurp the powers of the judiciary.
9. The test of police efficiency is the absence of crime and disorder, not the visible evidence of police action in dealing with it.

Increased crime and disorder after the Second World War led to increased demands for police intervention, with increased telephone ownership providing greater public access to the police and personal radios the means to deploy officers. To cope with increased demand, a 1967 Home Office Circular proposed 'unit beat policing' (UBP), with officers being deployed in cars to cover a wider geographic patrol area. The intention was that they should park up and patrol on foot in a number of different localities during their shift while at the same time being able to respond to calls. Arguably, UBP distanced the police from communities.

Problem-oriented policing

US sociologist Hermen Goldstein argued that prevention was best achieved through tackling the causes of crime in collaboration with the community. Police, he argued, had lost sight of their purpose, becoming obsessed with procedure. To provide a more structured approach, he established the concept of problem-oriented policing (POP).

PROBLEM-ORIENTED POLICING

1   It prevents and controls conduct that threatens life and property.
2   It assists victims and vulnerable citizens.
3   It initiates conflict resolution within the community.
4   It identifies emerging problems before they become crises.
5   It reduces fear of crime.

It achieves this by:

- defining problems with greater specificity
- researching the problem
- exploring alternative solutions
- reviewing interventions

Zero tolerance policing

In an article first published in 1982, Wilson and Kelling (reproduced in Newburn (ed.), 2005) advocated that crime was more likely in areas of decay and deprivation ('broken windows' thesis) and that swift community-based intervention to resolve minor issues (e.g. graffiti, abandoned cars) would keep major crime (street drugs, burglary) away. This has been termed 'zero tolerance' (ZT) policing.

ZERO TOLERANCE POLICING

1   Strict enforcement measures against minor crime ensure that more serious crime is kept out of the neighbourhood (crime control thesis).
2   There is little room for discretion.
3   It requires a partnership approach (cleaning graffiti, removing cars, repairing windows).
4   It is resource intensive.

Total geographic policing

Notwithstanding Commissioner Newman's experimentation with POP in London in the 1980s, POP and ZT enjoyed only episodic consideration in the UK. Police disengagement with communities was evident not only through vehicle patrolling and a focus on response to calls, but also from urban unrest in the 1980s. Lord Scarman, in analysing the causes of the Brixton riots, asserted that if police were faced with having to choose between preserving the peace or prosecuting crimes, priority should be given to community peace preservation, even if that means not investigating or prosecuting some crimes. To re-engage the police and communities, the Home Office experimented with Total Geographic Policing (TGP).

TOTAL GEOGRAPHIC POLICING

1   Also called 'sector' or 'neighbourhood' policing.
2   Dedicated community policing teams are responsible for small geographic localities rather than functional specialisms.
3   Working patterns are tailored to community needs rather than following traditional station-/shift-based policing.
4   There is an emphasis on consultation with other agencies.

Intelligence-led policing

TGP, where piloted, failed to achieve the reductions in crime and increased sense of safety that were anticipated. At the same time there was growing police concern that crime investigation was now very much second-place to community policing. In an attempt to enhance the status and skills of crime investigation and marry these to better informed resource deployment and community problem-solving, senior detectives advocated intelligence-led policing (ILP), arguing that more sophisticated crime management would lead to safer communities.

INTELLIGENCE-LED POLICING

1   The majority of volume crime is committed by only a few criminals, therefore focus on the criminal not the crime.
2   The police increasingly use intelligence to tackle problems proactively rather than reactively.

(Continued)

> *(Continued)*
>
> 3 The National Intelligence Model (NIM) provides a business framework for prioritisation.
> 4 It aims to disrupt criminality before it happens; there is effective enforcement against crimes committed.
> 5 There is a greater reliance on information technology to process intelligence.

Neighbourhood policing

ILP enjoyed Home Office endorsement in the National Policing Plan 2003–08, which required English and Welsh police forces to implement the NIM by April 2004. Notwithstanding the detectives' rationale underpinning ILP, the government White Paper *Building Communities, Beating Crime* envisages the NIM as part of the foundation for a return to community-focused, neighbourhood policing, which the Home Office argues is necessary as part of police reform for the twenty-first century. Neighbourhood policing (in its twenty-first century form) seeks to achieve community reassurance in an era when crime is falling but fear of crime is rising.

> **THE BLAIR GOVERNMENT'S VISION FOR TWENTY-FIRST-CENTURY NEIGHBOURHOOD POLICING**
>
> 1 It is citizen-focused.
> 2 It incorporates responsive neighbourhood (ward-based) policing teams: constables, PCSOs, wardens, special constables.
> 3 It is supported by wider partnerships to cut crime: CDRPs.
> 4 It is driven by strong police leadership and accountability.
> 5 It operates within a framework of national support, including better protective services and police reform.

> *Use original documents (e.g. government reports, empirical academic research papers) to identify who or what is driving a particular philosophy, and why and how it has been implemented. Don't just rely on the secondary literature.*

Risk management policing

A radically different interpretation of policing was asserted by Canadian sociologists Ericson and Haggerty. Viewing policing from a risk management perspective, they argue that the traditional view of policing (organised along military lines to protect persons and property within defined territories), articulated through law enforcement, order preservation and service provision, fails to acknowledge fully the way in which police knowledge contributes to wider regulation, security and governance in society.

RISK MANAGEMENT POLICING

1 Policing involves both intervention in citizens' lives and a response to an institutional need for knowledge about risks.
2 Community policing is risk communication.
3 Governance is dispersed throughout a number of institutions, agencies and private organisations.
4 Citizen coercion and compliance is embedded in social constructions and physical design and is not experienced as coercion at all.
5 Risk society is a knowledge society and the police are knowledge workers, sharing the knowledge they acquire with other managers of risk.
6 Surveillance, in all its forms (e.g. stop and search, CCTV, financial transaction monitoring), provides the routine production of knowledge of populations which is needed for their administration.

A number of questions arise from the philosophies presented above. Why have so many different philosophies emerged (since the 1960s)? To what extent do socio-political contexts determine the perceived need for, and define 'new' philosophies of, policing? How far, if at all, has policing philosophy departed from Peel's original principles? Do these principles still have relevance? Do community policing-based philosophies conflict with crime management philosophies (and vice versa)? To what extent are these individual philosophies implemented fully and exclusively either within individual forces or across the UK? How is the success of their practical implementation perceived?

❝ Compare and contrast the implications of zero tolerance policing and intelligence-led policing. ❞

After summarising the key points of zero tolerance and intelligence-led policing, the student could adopt either or both of the following possible approaches. What *resources*, both within the police service and among partner agencies, are required to give effect to each of these policing philosophies? What would be the *impact* on police relations with the community from each of these philosophies? The benefits and adverse consequences should be considered.

 Taking it **FURTHER**

What measures have been implemented (or laws enacted) to put these philosophies in place? And how successful were they? Case study material will be found in Newburn T (ed.) (2005) *Policing: Key Readings*, Cullompton: Willan, Part D; Dennis N (ed.) (1997) *Zero Tolerance: Policing a Free Society*, London: IEA Health & Welfare Unit; and Hale C et al. (2005) 'Uniform styles II: police families and policing styles', *Policing & Society* 15 (1), pp. 1–18.

Textbook Guide

FIELDING N (1995) *Community Policing*, Oxford: Oxford University Press

HOME OFFICE (2004) *Building Communities, Beating Crime*, Cm 6360, London: HMSO

NEWBURN T (ED.) (2005) *Policing: Key Readings*, Cullompton: Willan (ten papers in Part D)

TILLEY N (2003) 'Community policing, problem-oriented policing and intelligence-led policing', in T Newburn (ed.), *Handbook of Policing*, Cullompton: Willan, pp. 311–39

SCARMAN (LORD) (1981) *The Brixton Disorders, 10–12 April 1981: Report of an Inquiry*, London: HMSO

2.6
comparative policing

Core areas: **Public/private policing**
Different law enforcement agencies in any given nation
Policing function
Different models of policing

There are a number of areas in which comparative studies of policing can be undertaken: public policing/private security; different law enforcement agencies within a single jurisdiction; different types of police agency in different countries; policing philosophies (see section 2.5); policing functions/powers; and policing issues (crime control or public order preservation, policing by consent or policing dissent?). Mawby (2003) identifies legitimacy (including accountability), structure and function as key comparative criteria, and these criteria, which Mawby applies to different policing agencies in different jurisdictions, can be applied in any of the arenas identified above. This section identifies the plethora of issues prevailing in comparative studies. The questions posed illustrate the ways in which comparative studies can be taken further.

Running themes

Each of the running themes is pertinent to comparative studies between different policing systems: **police organisations** are structured differently; **police officers and staff** have different powers and responsibilities; **victims, suspects, witnesses** and **third parties** are all treated differently, according to the different practices and domestic laws; the relationship between the police and **other agencies** (both public and private) will differ according to context; and **political perspectives** and the types and range of **statistical data** available will also be context-specific.

> Policing – its founding authority, statutory powers and functions – is jurisdiction, and therefore context-specific. Comparative analysis must take this into account.

Public/private policing

Within any given jurisdiction there is the dichotomy between public and private policing: what is the legitimacy, structure and function of any private policing provision in public spaces, for example? How does public satisfaction with private security compare with satisfaction with public policing provision? What is the relationship between public and private policing in different jurisdictions? How accountable is private policing provision compared to public policing?

Different law enforcement agencies in any given nation

Within the UK there are three criminal jurisdictions (England and Wales; Scotland; Northern Ireland), having between them 52 public police forces as well as a variety of other enforcement and regulatory agencies. How does policing compare between the three? Why is there a difference? Within England and Wales, for instance, how does the SOCA policing model compare with the shire force model? Why and how have the two models developed? What is the relationship between customs, immigration and the police?

Similarly, in France there is both a national gendarmerie accountable to the Ministry of Defence, and a national police (in urban areas) accountable to the Ministry of Justice. Beneath these two structures, some areas also have a third, municipal policing tier. In Belgium the gendarmerie and national police were recently merged. Why? To what problem was this the solution?

Where there are both state and federal agencies within a single country (e.g. Australia, Canada, Germany, the USA), how do their legitimacy, structure and function compare? What is the nature of their working relationship? In the USA, to which the UK is so often compared because of cultural affinities, there are six tiers of policing, often with overlapping geographical jurisdictions: federal, state, county, city, rural and special district (e.g. university police forces, the New York Port Authority Police). It is rarely possible to speak of a single-agency law enforcement framework within any given jurisdiction.

Policing function

In the UK jurisdictions, public police forces have identical functions, albeit that policing powers differ between the three jurisdictions. It cannot be assumed that policing functions are mirrored between different countries: different policing agencies often have different functions and powers, and either separate or overlapping geographical areas of responsibility. In France, for instance, the functions and powers of the gendarmerie and national police differ, and both of these differ from the functions and powers of the Compagnies Républicaines de Sécuritié (CRS) which focuses on public order rather than on crime control, general community policing or administrative tasks. Policing function is often defined by the legal and social traditions of the relevant jurisdiction.

Different models of policing

Drawing upon Mawby's criteria, the table below summarises the basic characteristics of different models of policing. It should be emphasised that it is a basic guiding summary and that there will be local variation within each generic system.

" What are the key differences between policing in England and Scotland? "

One possible answer could be structured around the differences in procedural law, the different relationship between the police and other criminal justice professionals (such as the Crown Prosecution Service in England and the Procurator in Scotland), and the relationship and structure of forces.

Taking it *FURTHER*

A useful area for further exploration is the relationship between public and private policing, especially in relation to the growing phenomenon of gated communities or in areas where local residents have hired their own private security. For instance, does the presence of private policing generate more work for the public police?

System	Legitimacy	Structures	Function
UK	Based in statute, policing by public consent; citizens in uniform; democratic accountability articulated through police authorities, lay visitor schemes, public consultation Independent from prosecutors	SOCA – national agency, and Northern Ireland provincial agency, otherwise local policing delivery at shire and metropolitan level	Preserving the sovereign's peace; crime control; and, arguably, occasionally enforcing government policy (e.g. policing the miners' strike, 1984)
Continental Europe	Accountable to government ministries Less public accountability because of central government control and working relationship with investigating judiciary and prosecutors who oversee police investigations	Generally more centralised and militaristic than UK models National gendarmeries are sometimes supplemented by local policing provision. Alternatively, primary policing provision is at canton/regional level, supplemented by specialist provision at a national level	Crime control; public order; political and administrative functions
USA	Federal, state, county or city laws, or special jurisdictions based on geography or function Accountability to the law and Constitution although city police commissioners and sheriffs are often directly elected (and therefore susceptible to political influence)	Government agency working to the Department of Justice; state/city agency working to state/city authorities; Estimated 17–19,000 police forces, some with ten or fewer staff	Crime control; community policing; historical mistrust of federal agencies and centralised control has fostered tradition of minimal federal authority
Canada	National government and state government	Royal Canadian Mounted Police provide national policing functions; state policing functions in two states and support state police in other areas	Crime control; public order

(Continued)

System	Legitimacy	Structures	Function
Australia	Commonwealth (federal) and state laws	Australian Federal Police with limited authority in the states; states/territory police forces; special (permanent) Commissions of Inquiry for specific criminality (e.g. New South Wales Crime Commission; Australian Securities and Investments Commission)	Criminal justice and law enforcement is a state/territory function; Commonwealth authority focuses on limited Commonwealth criminal offences
Soviet and post-soviet societies	Legitimacy derived from working for the People and with the Party Both Russia and China had versions of local community crime control initiatives although under Stalin Russian police assumed a totalitarian authority Post-soviet policing has tended to focus on crime control rather than the democratisation of policing	Highly centralised both before and after communism	Crime control and political suppression during the communist era although Chinese police also have social welfare functions
Colonial and post-colonial societies	Derived from colonial occupation; little or no account taken of indigenous views Post-colonial democratic regimes have tended to retain centralised policing authority	Militaristic and centralised	Subjugation of indigenous peoples and administrative support for colonial powers Post-colonial regimes have often found it useful to retain the colonial policing functions in relation to administrative support alongside crime control and public order

(Continued)

System	Legitimacy	Structures	Function
Japan	Imported European continental models after centuries of family/feudal social control Local accountability more theoretical than effective	National police agency divided into prefectures	Crime control; public order
Islamic societies	Originally, Shari'a law based on Divine authority articulated through the Qu'ran Subsequently modified when western colonial powers (including the British) imposed Napoleonic inquisitorial model of criminal justice Resurgent Shari'a movement based on modified, inquisitorial model	Originally, a judicial inquiry into individual complaint (no police, no pre-trial investigation) Colonial and post-colonial: centralised, authoritarian and militaristic policing	Maintenance of societal stability in accordance with Divine law

Textbook guide

DONNELLY D & SCOTT, K (2005) *Policing Scotland, Cullompton, Willan*

JEFFERSON T (1990) *The Case against Paramilitary Policing, Milton Keynes: Open University Press*

JOHNSTON L (1992) *The Rebirth of Private Policing, London: Routledge*

JONES T & NEWBURN T (1998) *Private Security and Public Policing, Oxford: Oxford University Press*

MAWBY R (2003) *'Models of policing', in T Newburn (ed.), Handbook of Policing, Cullompton: Willan, pp. 15–40*

MULCAHY A (2005) *Policing Northern Ireland, Cullompton: Willan*

VOGLER R (2005) *A World View of Criminal Justice, Aldershot: Ashgate*

2.7	
International and transnational policing	

Core areas: **International policing**
Transnational policing

There is an important distinction between international and transnational policing.

International policing   'Peace support' missions (sometimes in conjunction with the military) under the auspices of the United Nations or European Union, or by national government invitation (e.g. Kosovo, East Timor, Iraq)
      Assistance and training provided to enhance specific capabilities (e.g. support to applicant and accession states to the EU provided by member states; US International Law Enforcement Academies in Budapest and Bangkok)

Transnational policing   The investigation of cross-border criminality offending national criminal laws by domestic police agencies either individually or in joint operations with agencies from other national jurisdictions (e.g. drugs-trafficking)

Running themes

International and transnational policing engage with the running themes in different ways. International policing often involves the establishment and development of **police organisations** in destabilised or emerging states whereas in transnational policing the focus is on co-operation between different national agencies. **Victims**, **suspects** and **witnesses** tend not to feature so much in international policing issues but are all relevant in transnational policing. **Political perspectives** are influenced not only by policing policy but also by international relations. The family of **other agencies** collaborating with police in the international arena differs from that in the transnational arena, and both differ from inter-agency co-operation and partnership policing in the domestic arena. The **wider community**, as used in the discussion of domestic or local policing, tends not to be either aware or particularly interested in international or transnational policing issues which itself begs questions about where the authority and legitimacy of both international and transnational policing originate.

> ***Common pitfalls:*** Confusing the terms international and transnational policing in essays and exam answers will lose marks. Failing to acknowledge the key differences between different types of jurisdiction and legal tradition, which define domestic policing, will suggest to the examiner that the candidate does not fully appreciate the complexity of context within which transnational and international policing takes place.

International policing

International policing activity seeks to support the stabilisation of chaotic or emerging states and the restoration/enhancement of democratic government through the promotion of policing norms. In the case of states wishing to join the European Union (EU), they must achieve certain policing and justice standards before they will be admitted and the authorities in existing member states provide training and advisers to help applicant states achieve the required standards.

But an important question arises. Since, by definition, assistance is intended to change the nature of policing in the assisted state, how well will the policing culture of the assistance provider translate into a new cultural environment? Do the foreign policy interests of the providing state coincide with the domestic interests of the assisted state?

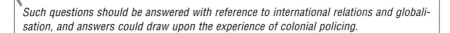

> *Such questions should be answered with reference to international relations and globalisation, and answers could draw upon the experience of colonial policing.*

Transnational policing

National legislatures define criminal law. There is no international criminal code, although war crimes, genocide, crimes against humanity, and crimes of aggression are considered universally to be so heinous that the UN International Criminal Court (ICC) exists to put suspects on trial in circumstances where national courts cannot or will not do so.

Transnational policing tackles cross-border criminality that falls outside the ICC remit: the trafficking of drugs, humans and arms, and the laundering of criminal profits, for instance. These constitute offences against the criminal laws of individual nation states and are investigated and prosecuted by the authorities in individual states as they would investigate crimes committed entirely within their own borders.

The last half-century witnessed a significant and continuing growth in transnational crime, mostly organised in nature and commercial in scope. With increasing frequency investigating authorities find that key evidence is located abroad and must be brought back to their own jurisdiction in order to be put on or used in trial. The repatriation of suspects is called *extradition*; the process by which evidence can be obtained from abroad and criminal assets located abroad can be seized is called *mutual legal assistance*.

The principle of national sovereignty and jurisdiction dictates that police agents from one state have no authority to exercise their domestic powers in the territory of another state. Limited exceptions to this principle are set out in inter-governmental treaties, which have to be given domestic effect within the jurisdictions of signatory parties that seek consensus on what constitutes criminal behaviour and provide mechanisms for assistance between different national police agencies.

Examples of inter-governmental treaties

European Convention on Mutual Assistance in Criminal Matters 1959 (Council of Europe)

Schengen Convention for the Gradual Abolition of Border Controls (Title III – Police and Security) 1995 (EU)

Convention between the Member States on Mutual Assistance in Criminal Matters 2000 (EU)

Convention against Transnational Organised Crime 2000 (UN)

Convention on Cybercrime 2001 (Council of Europe)

These treaties enable investigating authorities to request and provide assistance in, among other matters, obtaining witness statements, searching for property and conducting covert surveillance. The EU Schengen Convention allows police agencies from one member state to conduct surveillance operations in the territory of another with permission and, in relation to uniform policing, allows hot pursuit of escaping suspects or prisoners across land borders (the UK has not entered into the 'hot pursuit' element of the Schengen Convention and has its own cross-border arrangements with Eire, the only EU state with which the UK shares a land border). The EU also has a framework for allowing Joint Investigation Teams (JIT) to be established, based in one country but to which police officers from other participating authorities will be seconded. JITs are established on a case-by-case basis.

Three key international institutions have been established to facilitate transnational policing. These are:

- Interpol (1923, reconstituted 1956)   Association of police agencies from 178 states. No operational powers. Exists to facilitate exchange of information and requests between police agencies. Headquarters in Lyon. (www.interpol.int)
- Europol (1995)   EU institution, founded upon an inter-governmental treaty. No operational powers. Identifies and exchanges strategic intelligence on crime across the EU and operational intelligence in support of joint investigations involving two or more member states. Headquarters are in The Hague. (www.europol.eu.int)
- Eurojust (2002)   EU institution based in The Hague. Facilitates co-operation between prosecutors. (www.eurojust.eu.int)

A number of concerns prevail in the transnational policing arena. Different procedural laws in different national jurisdictions mean that investigators might be able to obtain evidence abroad that they could not lawfully obtain in their own jurisdiction. This is known as *process-laundering*. Protection of a suspect's rights in transnational policing is an important issue as, even within Europe, where nearly every state has signed the European Convertion on Human Rights (ECHR), rights protection varies between jurisdictions.

In inquisitorial tradition jurisdictions, the investigating magistrate seeks evidence relevant to the case, both incriminating and exculpatory. In adversarial jurisdictions, the prosecution presents only that evidence that will help its cause and so defendants, arguably, are at a disadvantage if there is no mechanism to enable them to secure evidence from abroad in their defence. Suspects in England and Wales can seek help from the courts in this, but the USA, as a point of principle, denies suspects any access to mutual legal assistance and will not respond to defence requests from the UK.

Whereas national policing is characterised by direct enforcement of domestic criminal law, transnational policing is characterised by assistance networks and mechanisms that facilitate domestic investigations with a cross-border element. International policing, on the other hand, must be viewed within the context of international relations and politics.

❝Do Europol and Interpol complement or compete with each other?❞

One possible approach would be to outline the different constitutional bases and remits of the two organisations and discuss this question in terms of function and accountability. Alternatively, an answer might focus on the area of the European Union where both organisations operate, considering whether there is benefit for EU member states in being members of both organisations.

Taking it **FURTHER**

Arguably, transnational policing suffers a democratic deficit. This can be explored in two ways. What *protections* exist for suspects in a transnational investigation? How *accountable* is transnational policing? And to whom? Relevant secondary material will be found in Gane C & Mackarel M (1996). 'The admissibility of evidence obtained from abroad into criminal proceedings – the interpretation of mutual legal assistance treaties and use of evidence irregularly obtained', *European Journal of Crime, Criminal Law & Criminal Justice* 4, pp. 98–119. Also in the thematic issue of *Policing & Society*, 12 (4), 2002, which focuses on police accountability in Europe.

Textbook guide

ANDERSON M ET AL. (1995) *Policing the European Union, Oxford: Oxford University Press*

ANDREAS P & NADELMANN E (2006) *Policing the Globe: Criminalization and Crime Control in International Relations, Oxford: Oxford University Press*

DEFLEM M (2002) *Policing World Society, Oxford: Oxford University Press*

REICHEL P (ED.) (2005) *The Handbook of Transnational Crime and Justice, London: Sage*

SHEPTYCKI J (ED.) (2000) *Issues in Transnational Policing, London: Routledge*

2.8
partnership and police reform

Core areas: **Specialist police forces**
Police staff and special constables
Partnership
Police reform and the future of policing
Performance and accountability
Workforce modernisation
Force restructuring
The new policing
The revolving door of reform

Policing functions are not confined to the police. For instance, Schedule 1, Regulation of Investigatory Powers Act (RIPA) 2000 lists all the public authorities that may use covert surveillance pursuant to their regulatory/enforcement functions, illustrating the extent of policing activity. The recent concept of the 'extended police family' encompasses agencies or agents who directly assist police forces (specialist police forces, police staff and special constables, and policing partnerships), rather than all authorities with regulatory or enforcement powers. Partnership based on the extended police family is part of a wider police reform programme initiated by Tony Blair's government.

Running themes

Perhaps the most important of the different perspectives to bear in mind when considering the new drive towards policing by partnership is that of the **other agencies** who will work with the police in Crime and Disorder Partnerships, for instance. But the success of partnership working will depend upon attitudes among **police officers and staff**. The **wider community** will have differing views both on partnership working, depending upon what they get out of it and how visible it is, and on the reform of the **police organisation**. But the reform agenda is not merely about restructuring police forces. It is also about reshaping the workforce with new skills and new types of role to deliver partnership policing and so directly affects **police officers and staff**. Home Office attempts to achieve force restructuring in 2005/06 were founded upon the **political perspective** that, ever since the last phase of major restructuring ended in 1974, there still remain too many police forces for there to be real efficiency and economies of scale. Performance **statistics** in part inform this view.

Specialist police forces

Police forces can be broadly divided into two types: the public forces (sometimes called Home Department forces) and private forces (or non-Home Department forces). Public forces – the Metropolitan Police Service, the City of London and the 41 county forces in England and Wales – are defined in Section 1 and Schedule 1, Police Act 1996.

Some geographical locations fell outside the remit of the nineteenth-century borough and county forces. Railways and canals, for instance, could traverse many different policing jurisdictions and so the private companies running these transport routes were empowered by Parliament to appoint their own Constables or Special Constables. Hence the Stockton & Darlington Railway had its own police force from circa 1825, and the London–Birmingham Railway had its own police force from 1833. The Port Authorities of Liverpool and London were among the many dockyard authorities empowered to establish police forces.

From these arose the concept of functionally specialist police forces with limited geographical jurisdictions: the British Transport Police (BTP, which came into its current form with railway nationalisation in 1949), the British Atomic Energy Authority Police (the first fully armed police force in the UK now reconstituted as the Civil Nuclear Constabulary), the Ministry of Defence Police (not to be confused with the military police forces – the Royal Military Police, the RAF Police and the Royal Navy Provost Marshall). Outside their geographical area of jurisdiction, these forces usually have Special Constabulary status. Within their jurisdiction, however, they have not only full police powers but also additional powers not available to public forces. There has been a gradual reduction and consolidation of these private forces. For instance, the Serious Organised Crime and Police (SOCAP) Act 2005 abolished the Royal Parks Constabulary, incorporating it within the MPS. In many ports, private police forces were replaced initially by BTP, and subsequently by private security.

The Thatcher administration's drive towards privatisation saw the creation of a private municipal borough force in London – Wandsworth

Parks Police – to police growing problems of crime and anti-social behaviour in 70 open spaces within Wandsworth Borough comprising some 850 acres. Their precise legal status and authority is disputed (see Jones & Newburn 1998, p. 132) and clearly begs questions about how such a force interacts with the public police within whose police area they coincide. The Boroughs of Greenwich, Kensington and Chelsea, and Hammersmith and Fulham have also established parks police forces.

Police staff and special constables

Striving for ever-greater public sector efficiency, the Conservative administration (1979–97) pursued 'civilianisation' of police posts, intending to replace police officers performing non-operational roles with non-police officers, to enable the redeployment of police officers to operational roles requiring full police powers.

An early example of a delegated policing function to non-police officers is that of the traffic warden, whose responsibilities focus on ensuring free-flowing traffic. In many areas parking attendants employed by local councils are replacing traffic wardens employed by the local police force. The media often relay the perception that this is no more than an income-generation strategy for local councils (through parking fines), but despite the vociferous outcry against such measures there is evidence that the proliferation and presence of parking attendants on the streets contributes to a reduction in crime and disorder because of their uniformed presence.

Since 1997, the Labour government has taken 'civilianisation' further, arguing that not all operational roles necessarily require full police powers and that some investigative functions, for instance statement-taking from witnesses and basic patrolling, could be invested in civilian police staff, thus releasing more sworn constables for functions requiring full police powers. Civilian police staff are less costly to employ than sworn constables, and this was seen as the most cost-effective means of addressing the twin demands of responding to the ever-increasing number of incident-specific calls to the police while at the same time providing a more visible presence for the purposes of preventing minor disorder and petty crime.

The Police Reform Act 2002, Part 4 and Schedule 4, empowered chief constables to designate non-police officers with the powers to be:

- a police community support officer (PCSO)
- an investigator

- a detention officer
- an escort officer.

Of these, the most controversial is the role of PCSOs, which the Police Federation argues is policing on the cheap and represents two-tier policing. The exact nature of a PCSO's powers is a matter for individual chief officers to designate and the extent to which police forces have utilised PCSOs is as varied as the powers invested in them. The SOCAP Act 2005, section 122, empowered chief officers to designate PCSOs with powers of detention, using reasonable force if necessary, if they attend an incident requiring the presence of a constable, and to issue fixed penalty notices for, among other offences, disorder.

Special constables, that is citizens undertaking police duty with full powers on a part-time, unpaid basis, are of greater antiquity than the modern incarnation of constable. They preserve the medieval concept of a citizen's civic responsibility for policing. Each police force has a special constabulary whose members generally perform uniform duties, supplementing full-time officers. Both the full-time police and the public express concerns about the professionalism of the part-time police, but their political advantage lies in boosting, and therefore meeting public demand for, a greater visible police presence.

Partnership

The police cannot solve all the problems presented to them. Many problems can be more appropriately resolved by other agencies. The Crime and Disorder Act 1998 requires the police and local councils to work together to produce crime and disorder strategies to guide the work of Crime and Disorder Reduction Partnerships (CDRPs) (Crime and Disorder Act 1998, s. 5; amended by Police Reform Act 2002, s. 97).

Section 40 of the Police Reform Act 2002 extended the partnership family by creating Community Safety Accreditation Schemes. These are intended to foster closer partnership working and information-sharing in order to tackle anti-social behaviour. Chief police officers can accredit non-police employees working in a community safety role with a limited range of police powers similar to those of PCSOs. Those who can be accredited include neighbourhood wardens, security guards, park rangers, hospital and university security staff, fire and rescue service personnel, housing association employees, environmental health officers and parking attendants. Such schemes are operating or planned in over half of police force areas in England and Wales.

Powers available to PCSOs and accredited persons, pursuant to the Police Reform Act 2002, Schedules 4 and 5, the Anti-Social Behaviour Act 2003, s.33, and the SOCAP Act 2005, Schedule 8)

- Issue fixed penalty notices for riding on a footway, dog fouling, littering, graffiti, fly-posting and truancy, and for a range of disorder offences, including alcohol-related offences and fireworks offences
- Require names and addresses from persons whom the accredited person believes has committed a relevant fixed penalty offence or an offence that causes injury, alarm or distress or loss of or damage to property, and of a person acting in an anti-social manner, and for certain traffic offences
- Confiscate alcohol from persons drinking in a designated public place and from under-18s, and tobacco from under-16s
- Require the removal of abandoned vehicles
- Stop vehicles for testing
- Control traffic for the purpose of escorting abnormal loads and other purposes
- Stop cycles for the purposes of issuing a fixed penalty notice
- Deal with begging and request name and address
- Photograph persons away from the police station who have been given a fixed penalty notice
- It is also an offence to assault or wilfully obstruct an accredited person in his or her duty.

At the other end of the policing scale (dealing with organised crime on a national and transnational level), government opted away from partnership by merging the National Crime Squad (NCS), the National Crime Intelligence Service (NCIS) and the investigative departments of Her Majesty's Customs and Excise (HMCE) and Her Majesty's Immigration Service (HMIS), together with intelligence specialists from MI5, into the new Serious Organised Crime Agency (SOCA). SOCA is not a police force but its staff will be designated with the powers of either a constable, a customs officer and immigration officer or any permutation of these, as the SOCA Director-General deems necessary.

The extended police family is changing the relationship between the police and the community. The Home Office (2004) envisages police constables managing neighbourhood policing teams comprising PCSOs and accredited wardens. It could be argued that having delegated to the new nineteenth-century professional police, the citizen's responsibility for policing his or her own community, the demands on the professional police for policing crime have now become so great that responsibility for policing community peace has had to be restored to the community with wardens and PCSOs assuming roles once undertaken by nightwatchmen and parish constables.

Police reform and the future of policing

> Section 4.2 in this volume itemises key legislation and official reports concerning the purpose, function and constitution of policing in England and Wales. In doing so, it provides a record of reformation.

It is not so very far-fetched to suggest that policing has been in a state of perpetual reform since the early nineteenth century when the first public police forces were established. There is no great surprise in this. Society is continuously changing and therefore the demands of policing society inevitably change.

What has been witnessed in the last quarter-century is an increase in the political interest in police reform, which stems from law and order becoming an election issue in 1979 and which became embedded with Conservative public sector reform in the interests of economy, efficiency and effectiveness. Much of the earlier reform focused on force structures and jurisdictions, and to some extent policing function. From the 1980s onwards, the focus was primarily on service delivery and reducing costs. From time to time, notably in the annual Dimbleby Lecture given in 2005 by Metropolitan Police Commissioner Sir Ian Blair, the question 'what is policing for?' has been raised, reflecting concerns that policing may not be responding to societal change. It is not always apparent that this question has been answered before reforms have been initiated.

Key thinker

THE DESBOROUGH COMMITTEE report, 1919, is a useful benchmark for police reform in the twentieth century.

Performance and accountability

There are two key facets of this topic: officer behaviour and force management. The former came under close scrutiny during the 1970s and 1980s, with high-profile miscarriages of justice leading to a statutory clarification of police powers and a requirement for police to become more transparent through documentation (Police and Criminal Evidence Act (PACE) 1984)

The second facet entered the spotlight when Prime Minister Thatcher's New Public Management of the 1980s was applied to the police service in the 1990s following a series of Audit Commission papers. The Sheehy Inquiry (1993) reviewed police pay and conditions and made a number of radical recommendations, applying private sector management logic to the police service. Initially endorsed by the then Home Secretary, Michael Howard, the report was shelved within a few months following widespread police opposition. Elements of it nevertheless found their way into the 1993 White Paper (Cm 2281) and subsequently into the Police and Magistrates Court Act 1994 (subsequently consolidated with the 1964 Act in the Police Act 1996) which went some way to redefine the tripartite relationship.

Sheehy's remit omitted the function of the police. Functionality was reviewed independently by Posen (1996), who concluded that there were some functions that could be devolved from the police service to other providers but that essentially the services provided by the police (as opposed to their enforcement functions) were key to the overall success of the police and their relations with the policed.

Through the setting of national policing priorities, a more robust HMIC inspection regime, and the statutory requirement to achieve 'best value', the Home Office has driven innovation nationally in police performance management in a way that individual police authorities could not have achieved. The most recent culmination of the performance innovations has been the introduction of the Police Performance Assessment Framework (PPAF) and Baseline Assessments, against 27 areas of policing activity, which has enabled comparisons not only between forces but between BCUs as the government strives to ensure that BCUs, rather than forces, are the lynchpin of local policing delivery.

Workforce modernisation

Sheehy's ill-fated inquiry was the first attempt at police workforce modernisation in the modern period. It focused on rank and pay structure (including performance-related pay) in a carrot-and-stick approach to driving down salary costs while driving up performance efficiency. A more subtle approach to reducing salary costs has been the increasing civilianisation of policing, that is the gradual replacement of sworn police officers by non-sworn police staff who are paid considerably less than officers. This initiative has been reinforced by the delegation of police functions, and latterly some police powers as well, to new members of the 'extended police family', such as PCSOs. The development of this initiative is documented in the White Papers of 2001 and 2004 (see Section 4.2).

Force restructuring

The merger of small police forces into larger entities has been a perpetual theme throughout British policing history. The emphasis on local policing provision, coupled with the fact that a national police force historically has been anathema to politicians and public alike (having witnessed the political role played by national police forces in nineteenth-century continental Europe), meant that the creation of the first public police forces resulted in the proliferation of many very small organisations. Inevitably, economies of scale, together with central government's desire for a greater influence over the quality of policing provision, have driven mergers, often in phases, the latest of which was abandoned after only ten months in June 2006.

In the 1960s there were two phases of mergers following first the Royal Commission on Policing (1960–62) and then the Royal Commission on Local Government (1969). In combination, these mergers reduced the number of forces in England and Wales to 43. The 2005–06 debate on whether these should be further amalgamated into regional forces was initiated following a review of police capability against regional and national measures as opposed to the local measures against which forces have traditionally be assessed. This review, published in an HMIC report, *Closing the Gap* (2005), concluded that for regional and national policing needs, local forces were 'not fit for purpose'. The conclusion that structures designed for one purpose are not best suited for delivering another purpose superficially is not revolutionary, but given local political sensitivities about the 'ownership' of policing, the government's decision to merge forces as a solution to the problems identified (although this was not the only solution considered by the HMIC) was seen by many, particularly police authorities, as radical and objectionable. The position of chief constables in this debate is interesting, with some supporting merger publicly, others publicly opposing merger and others publicly opposing (and so being seen to agree with their police authorities) but privately favouring merger. A change in Home Secretary (June 2006) resulted in the indefinite postponement of restructuring, leaving 43 forces in England and Wales in limbo to find their own solutions.

This quandary epitomises the dichotomy between the desire for local control of policing and the need for policing responses that transcend force boundaries.

The new policing

SOCA is an example both of new policing approaches and workforce modernisation. It is a response to the perceived need for new structures and new approaches to dealing with organised crime (Home Office 2004c). SOCA's approach will be focused as much on the disruption and dismantling of organised business and networks as upon traditional crime detection. Organised crime is notoriously difficult to measure, which begs the question, in terms of performance management, how will SOCA's success be judged?

Innovative, partnership solutions are also being sought at the other end of the policing continuum – neighbourhood-based policing teams comprising constables, PCSOs, street wardens and others. Arguably, the success of these teams will be easier to illustrate.

The revolving door of reform

One characteristic of the current Labour government is its public sector reform crusade, resulting in the early abandonment of recent innovations. Hence the NCS and NCIS, both initiatives of Conservative governments, became operational in 1998, were reconstituted in 2001, and merged into SOCA in 2006. National Police Training was reconstituted as Centrex in 2001, to which were subsequently appended the National Centre for Policing Excellence and the National Specialist Law Enforcement Centre. Together with the Police Information and Technology Organisation (PITO, established 1998), these are now to be disbanded and merged into the National Policing Improvement Agency (NPIA). At the same time as forces were having to think through potential mergers and comprehensive restructuring, the national provision of probationer training was abolished and responsibility for probationer training was devolved back to forces. The concept of a National Policing Plan, enshrined in statute in 2002, was reconfigured as a National Community Safety Plan in 2006.

Police powers are also under constant review, with PACE being amended in 2001 and again in 2005. At time of writing, RIPA is also being reviewed.

❝ What would be the advantages and disadvantages of implementing Sir Ian Blair's controversial suggestion in 2005 to incorporate the BTP establishment located within London's railways and Underground into the MPS? ❞

The answer must be set in the context of the regionalisation debate (2005–06) and must draw upon Ian Blair's Dimbleby Lecture (2005). What would be lost/gained by transferring a specialist transport police function to a public police force? Would the same arguments apply elsewhere or are the circumstances in London unique?

❝ Police authorities have statutory responsibility for maintaining efficient and effective police forces. What consequences, if any, have arisen for the tripartite relationship from Home Office-driven police performance management initiatives? ❞

Any tripartite relationship question will be exploring the balance of power within the relationship as well as the arguments for and against local versus central control of policing. This question, in particular, is inviting discussion about the relative autonomy of police authorities to determine policing priorities.

Taking it ***FURTHER***

This is a topic replete with opportunities for further study, dissertation and research projects.

Civilianisation and delegation of policing functions is premised upon the argument that not all policing activity has to be undertaken by persons with the powers of a constable. Critics argue that this is creating a second-class tier of policing provision. Is there any justification in the criticism?

What scope is there for co-ordination or conflict between the National Community Safety Plan, local policing plans and CDRP strategies?

The constable has been called a citizen in uniform: does the extension of the policing family and the extension of police powers to non-police staff (PCSOs, Accredited Persons, SOCA staff) alter the status of constable?

Textbook guide

HARFIELD C (2006) *'SOCA: a paradigm shift in British Policing', British Journal of Criminology 46, pp. 743–761*

HMIC (2005) *Closing the Gap, London: HMIC*

HOME OFFICE (2001) *Policing a New Century: A Blue-print for Reform, Cm 5326, London: HMSO*

HOME OFFICE (2004) *Building Communities, Beating Crime: A Better Police Service for the 21st Century, Cm 6360, London: HMSO*

JONES T & NEWBURN T (1998) *Private Security and Public Policing, Oxford: Oxford University Press*

NEWBURN T (ED.), (2005) *Policing: Key Readings, Cullompton: Willan, 8 Papers in Section F*

the practice of policing	

2.9	
policing public order	

Core areas: **Preserving order**
Policing public events
Policing disorder
Policing the miners' strike, 1984
Policing protest

Running themes

How do the demands on **police organisations** of policing public order differ from other policing demands? What are issues around welfare and training for **police**

officers and staff? How can the support of the **wider community** be won to diffuse potential public disorder (whether that be anti-social behaviour of violent protest), and what are the consequences for the community and **other agencies** of widescale disorder? What are the **politics** of policing public order?

There are two key aspects to this subject: *preserving public order* and *policing disorder*. The latter is required only when the former has failed.

Preserving order

The Blair government made the control of anti-social behaviour (i.e petty disorder at a neighbourhood level, including rowdy behaviour and minor crime such as vandalism) a political priority. To reinforce the role of uniform patrol as a disorder deterrent, the role of police community support others (PCSOs) has been created and control mechanisms supplemented by Anti-Social Behaviour Orders that seek to constrain individuals causing a nuisance.

Policing public events

Legislation exists that requires event organisers to notify the police in advance of an event such as a protest or demonstration. If organizers reglect to do so, the police can veto a proposed event. However, primarily, police duty in relation to events is to ensure that those taking place in public spaces are safe.

Police core responsibilities in relation to (non-commercial) events in public places include:

- *Prevention and detection of crime*
- *Prevention or stopping breaches of the peace*
- *Traffic regulation within the legal powers provided by statute, a Road Closure Order or a Traffic Regulation Order*
- *Activation of a contingency plan where there is an immediate threat to life and the co-ordination of resultant emergency service activities.*

What has been seen traditionally as policing activity at public events is now often delivered by the private security sector. Alternatively, the police charge for their services at such events. This privatisation of policing is conducted in partnership with the police. During 2005, the Metropolitan

Police Service Public Order branch was involved in co-ordinating more than 3,500 events, very few of which descended into serious disorder.

Policing disorder

Policing public disorder, that is restoring order and peace, is very different from other policing tasks. Images are evoked of riot-clad officers engaged in forceful confrontation and with a battery of tools at their disposal, including truncheons, CS gas, shields, dogs and horses. However, the police spend considerable time in ensuring that disorder is avoided so that confrontation and outbreaks are relatively rare.

Policing public disorder has decreased significantly since the late nineteenth century, although there has been a slight increase in the last 25 years. The general historical trend from the nineteenth to twentieth century has been a transformation from 'stoning and shooting' strikes to 'pushing and shoving' strikes, accompanied by a progressively less coercive police response. The first time police officers (excluding Northern Ireland) were shot during public disorder was at the Tottenham riots in 1985. Typically, ensuring public order today involves a range of activities from policing sports events to major demonstrations and protests. Nonetheless, policing public disorder is politically contentious as it is a highly visible and symbolic representation of the relationship between the state and citizen.

The sectarian Troubles in Northern Ireland were unique within the UK. The Patten Report (1999) identified that public order policing failings in the 1960s were partly responsible for the Troubles of the following 30 years, and for deepening nationalist estrangement from the then Royal Ulster Constabulary (RUC) (now the Police Service of Northern Ireland (PSNI)). There have been changes in public order policing since then, and today the PSNI are commended for their skilful police handling of potentially difficult public order events.

Policing the miners' strike, 1984

The iconic image created in policing disorder is that of the miners' strike (1984–85), which saw thousands of police from various forces deployed against miners, and frequently resulted in violent confrontation. The deployment of the police by the government, which included the establishment of an unprecedented national co-ordination centre, was politically motivated and the striking miners were referred to by Margaret Thatcher as 'the enemy within' who did not share the values of the British people.

Margaret Thatcher's close political ally, the former Conservative MP Nick Ridley, disclosed in his diaries that the Conservative party had been planning to provoke another miners' strike (in order to crush the National Union of Miners) ever since the strike of 1974 toppled the then Conservative government. As soon as they came to power in 1979, the new Conservative government began stock-piling coal and planning new legislation to utilise the police as a means of curbing trades union power.

Ridley N (1991) My Style of Government, London: Hutchinson

The government mobilised the police in large numbers to deal with picket lines on the grounds that they represented illegal intimidation and violence against those miners who wanted to go to work. During the industrial action 11,291 people were arrested and 8,392 were charged with offences such as breach of the peace and obstructing the highway. Former striking miners and others have alleged that soldiers of the British Army were dressed as policemen and used on the picket lines. While concrete evidence of this has not been produced (although film footage exists of 'policemen' wearing tunics without any identifying numbers on their lapels), it remains a point of contention today, and in many former mining areas antipathy towards the police remains strong. The government was criticised for abusing its power when it ruled that local police might be too sympathetic to the miners to take action against the strike, and instead brought in forces from distant counties.

Policing protest

The traditional approach to policing 'public order' reflected the experience of the serious urban violence of the 1980s and early 1990s. Strategies, tactics, training and equipment tended to concentrate on large events in the anticipation of violence and on the possibility of spontaneous outbreaks of large-scale disorder.

In recent years the nature of potential disorder has broadened. While violent protests still occur, less violent and non-violent protests have become more frequent. The involvement of a wider and better-informed representation of the public in single-cause protests, especially for political, environmental and animal rights issues, has witnessed the emergence of these new forms of protest. These have required the police to develop new tactics in order to manage them in a manner consistent with the concept of policing by consent and public expectations. In doing so they have to consider the democratic right of peaceful protest yet maintain a fine balance between the rights and responsibilities of protesters and those citizens not protesting. Lawful protests still have the potential to escalate into disorder, so while non-violent action calls for a sensitive, measured response from the police to ensure peace is maintained, it still requires the capability to respond quickly to the threat of violence should it arise.

"What lessons for policing were derived from the 1981 Brixton riots?"

A 'pass' answer will focus solely on the strategic and tactical lessons for public order policing. A better answer will additionally consider the lessons for community policing that are intended to prevent such future breakdowns in public order. Comparison with subsequent urban riots would illustrate whether the lessons have been learnt or whether there are new lessons to learn.

Taking it **FURTHER**

> The policing of sporting events, particularly football, has prompted strategic and tactical developments in public order policing. Consider the lessons from the Hillsborough and Bradford stadia disasters and what issues arise for town-centre policing during international football tournaments when pubs screen live matches.

Textbook guide

BUTTON M & JOHN T (2002) *'Plural policing' in action: a review of the policing of environmental protests in England and Wales'*, Policing & Society 12(2), pp. 111–21

FINE B & MILLAR R (1985) *Policing the Miners' Strike*, London: Lawrence & Wishart

HMIC (1999) *Keeping the Peace: Policing Disorder*, London: HMSO

SCARMAN LORD (1981) *The Brixton Disorders 10–12 April 1981*, Cmnd 8427 London: HMSO

2.10	
criminal investigation	

Core areas: **The authority to investigate**
Managing investigation
Intelligence-led investigation

There are two important areas to the study of criminal investigation, each linked to investigation quality. The first aspect is the legitimacy (including integrity) of investigation, the second concerns the practicalities of investigation management.

In terms of investigation management, volume crime and serious individual or serial crimes further complicate this subject area.

 Running themes

Legitimacy and practicalities predominate consideration of **police organisation** for criminal investigation, both for volume crime and for serious individual crimes. Likewise, different demands are made of **police officers and staff**. Students

should bear in mind the different vested interests and often conflicting perspectives of **victims**, **suspects**, and **witnesses** in relation to criminal investigation. The consequences for the **wider community**, **third parties** and **other agencies** should be considered. The extent to which the **political debate** about criminal investigation and its management is driven by **statistical data** must not be forgotten. Students should always consider whether the citation of any given statistical data really supports the political or academic argument being made with such data.

The authority to investigate

Prior to 1986, authority to search and arrest was contained within individual Acts, leading to a plethora of bespoke powers, the application of which was regulated by an informal set of guidelines called 'Judges Rules'. A series of high-profile miscarriages of justice (e.g. Guildford Four, Birmingham Six) and public disorder arising from the use of powers unique to the Metropolitan Police (e.g. Brixton riots), highlighted problems of professionalism and a lack of transparency and accountability in the conduct of criminal investigations, and led to a review of police powers and procedure.

Key statutes defining police powers and responsibilities

Police and Criminal Evidence Act 1984 (PACE) – stop and search, arrest, search of premises, custody, interview and identification procedures (much amended by subsequent legislation)

Criminal Procedures and Investigation Act 1996 (CPIA) – imposed an obligation on police to identify to the defence exculpatory evidence as well as securing incriminating evidence for the prosecution

Police Act 1997, Part III – interference with property for the purposes of covert investigation

Regulation of Investigatory Powers Act 2000 (RIPA) – covert surveillance, interception of communications, management of informants

---

PACE, which came into force in 1986, consolidated and revised basic police investigative powers. The Act is supplemented by seven Codes of

Practice which, while not having the force of law, nevertheless provide the context within which the fairness and professionalism of police investigation may be judged.

Key thinkers

Professor **Michael Zander** is the leading authority on PACE and his book, now in its fifth edition, is a key text (Zander 2005). However, PACE has been subsequently significantly amended by the SOCAP Act 2005.

Michael Mansfield's *Presumed Guilty: the British Legal System Exposed*, (co-author T Wardle, 1993) although dated, raises important issues about the practical implementation of PACE, questioning its effectiveness in regulating police behaviour.

The Human Rights Act (HRA) 1998 necessitated further review of police actions because hitherto covert investigation had been conducted merely on the basis that it was not illegal. The HRA meant that there had now to be specific statutory authority to undertake covert investigation. This was anticipated in the Police Act 1997 and underpinned the rationale for RIPA. Both these Acts sought to avoid prescribing warranted judicial authority for covert investigation in favour of police self-regulation through documented accountability – not a form of regulation that enjoys much confidence among civil liberties experts but a method that is more convenient for the police service.

There is considerable case law and literature on the use of police powers under PACE and a growing body of material about the use of covert investigation powers. On the one hand, there is the issue of securing sufficient evidence to ensure a successful prosecution of offenders on behalf of victims and wider society. On the other, is an issue of ensuring the rights of the suspect are not ignored or circumvented, thus undermining justice. Both views are different perspectives on ensuring the authority and integrity of the criminal justice system, which is a key criterion for a democratic society.

The academic journals Criminal Law Review and Covert Policing Review contain many useful papers on investigation powers

Managing investigation

Also related to quality is the management of criminal investigation, which itself divides into two categories: volume crime and serious crime; and reactive and proactive investigation. Responses in each case are defined by resource availability.

Limited police resources mean that volume crime has to be screened in order to maximise investigation efficiency. Low-value crimes to which there are no witnesses and for which there is no forensic evidence cannot be prosecuted and so are not investigated. Yet for the purposes of insurance claims and assessing insurance risk, such crimes are recorded (an example of the police working as knowledge workers for a non-police purpose). Hence police forces have resorted to crime management desks, as described in section 2.4.

Society demands that serious crime be investigated. Although murder investigation does not feature on any performance targets set for the police, it is unconscionable that such crimes should not be investigated. When such enquiries become protracted or especially complex (e.g. the Fred and Rosemary West serial murders; the Soham child murders; terrorist bombings) the drain on resources from other police activities is significant and detrimental. Securing appropriate capability for major crimes underlies arguments supporting proposals for police force regionalisation.

Information overload in the Yorkshire Ripper investigation (at least 13 murders and seven serious assaults between 1975 and 1981), which delayed the arrest of the offender and cost the lives of a number of victims, highlighted the need for computerised investigation support, and led to the creation of the Home Office Large Major Enquiry System (HOLMES, now updated to HOLMES2) for this purpose. Officers normally assigned to other tasks have to be specially trained and are used as an on-call reserve to populate HOLMES teams on an as-needed basis.

The increasing sophistication of forensic science is a double-edged sword for investigation management as evidence can now be secured in more ways but at an ever increasing cost. Obligations under the Criminal Procedure and Investigation Act 1996 (CPIA) mean that available forensic techniques must be explored but these carry a greater risk of procedural error, such as evidential contamination, which defence lawyers can use to cast doubt on the probity of prosecution evidence.

Intelligence-led investigation

The alternative to reactive investigation – investigation of reported crimes – is proactive or intelligence-led investigation against criminals identified as being active or crimes in action. This is used in two ways: for the investigation of organised crime, for which covert techniques are often required, in order secure evidence since such investigations rarely involve independent third-party witnesses to the crimes; and the targeting of prolific offenders involved in high-volume criminality through the application of a business management tool labelled the *National Intelligence Model* (NIM). Intelligence-led investigation, it is argued, facilitates the more efficient use of targeted resources.

Key thinkers

Sir David Phillips, **John Grieve** and **Brian Flood**, all senior police officers with considerable detective experience, pioneered intelligence-led policing in the 1990s. Their work was reinforced by two important reports: Audit Commission (1993) *Helping with Enquiries: Tackling Crime Effectively*, London: Audit Commission; HMIC (1999) *Policing with Intelligence*, London: HMIC.

The acquisition of intelligence, as much as evidential investigation, directly engages human rights issues, particularly when the intelligence needed has to be obtained by covert means. Thus this business-management approach further emphasises the need for good-quality investigation that can be appropriately reviewed and audited to ensure integrity of the process.

Although intelligence has always been crucial to successful criminal investigations, it is a skill area that the police service has only comparatively recently invested with specialist training and dedicated intelligence units. It is a complex area in which there are few certainties and many problems. It does not yet enjoy the same high career status within the police service as thief-taking.

"What contribution does the National Intelligence Model make to the management of criminal investigation?"

Understanding the NIM is key to understanding the relationship between local and cross-border crime and the various analytical and intelligence tools which inform prioritisation decisions when faced with more crime than investigation resources.

Taking it **FURTHER**

How have miscarriages of justice dictated changes in criminal procedure? Have changes in criminal procedure addressed all the concerns raised about police investigations in the 1970s and 1980s? The manner in which miscarriages and subsequent official reports have driven improvements in investigation powers and management is an area of fruitful further study.

So too is the issue of investigation resources: How does the resourcing of major enquiries adversely affect other policing activity?

What issues arise for the presentation at trial of evidence from a complex enquiry?

Textbook guides

ASHWORTH A (2002) *Human Rights, Serious Crime and Criminal Procedure,* London: Sweet & Maxwell

CLARK D (2004) *The Investigation of Crime (3rd edn),* London: Lexis Nexis Butterworth

FLOOD B (2004) *'Strategic aspects of the UK National Intelligence Model', in J Ratcliffe (ed.), Strategic Thinking in Criminal Intelligence,* Sydney: Federation Press, pp. 37–52

HARFIELD C & HARFIELD K (2005) *Covert Investigation,* Oxford: Oxford University Press.

MCCONVILLE M & WILSON G (EDS) (2002) *The Handbook of the Criminal Justice Process,* Oxford: Oxford University Press.

SANDERS A & YOUNG R (2000) *Criminal Justice, (2nd edn),* London: Butterworths

ZANDER M (2005) *The Police and Criminal Evidence Act (5th edn),* London: Sweet & Maxwell

2.11

policing and evidence

Core areas: **Role and responsibilities**
Regulation
Reliability
Resources

Running themes

How have **police organisations** responded to the need to gather reliable evidence? What training and specialist skills are required of **police officers and staff**? How do the different perspectives of **victims, suspects, witnesses** and the **wider community** contribute to our understanding of this topic? How have **other agencies**, particularly the courts, responded to the needs of these groups?

Criminal evidence is a vast topic on which much has been written, especially by legal scholars. For the introductory purposes of this volume, the subject of policing and evidence can be divided into four key themes:

- Role and responsibilities
- Regulation
- Reliability
- Resources

Role and responsibilities

No criminal trial can proceed without evidence. In the UK adversarial trial tradition, the onus of proof lies with the prosecution; the defence need not adduce evidence at trial at all if sufficient doubt can be cast upon the prosecution evidence. There are two integrity tests to be met. The *evidence* itself must be credible, of probative value and there must also be demonstrable integrity in the *processes* by which the evidence was secured. Evidence improperly obtained may be excluded from trial unless the court feels the evidence is of such relevance and value that it should be admitted.

In their role as primary gatherers of evidence for use at criminal trial, it is a police responsibility to ensure the integrity of the investigative procedures and the chain of evidential continuity between alleged crime and trial. This responsibility, in which the police act on behalf of the state and the wider community, is the foundation upon which police evidential powers and criminal procedural rules have been defined over time.

The adversarial principle prescribes that the accused should have the opportunity to cross-examine prosecution evidence at trial. Hence witness testimony is the preferred form of evidence although under certain circumstances documentary evidence may be adduced. The witness principle includes the presentation of forensic evidence: an expert witness will testify as to the nature of the forensic evidence. Assessment and interpretation of evidence is the role of the Crown Court jury or the lower court magistrate. Thus evidence presented must capable of interpretation by a layperson, not a legal professional.

The best available evidence will always be direct evidence: a witness to the crime being committed. In the absence of direct evidence, circumstantial evidence must be relied upon. The police must secure the best evidence available, and they have a legal obligation to disclose to the defence any evidence that tends to undermine the prosecution case or supports the defence case.

Direct evidence

Andy hears a commotion, enters the kitchen and sees Ben stab Colin with a knife.

Circumstantial evidence

Andy hears a commotion, enters the kitchen and sees Ben standing by Colin's dead body, which has a knife sticking out of it.

Regulation

Criminal procedural law regulates the manner in which police gather evidence.

Police and Criminal Evidence Act 1984 and Codes of Practice (as amended) – stop and search, arrest, custody procedures

Criminal Procedure and Investigation Act 1996 (as amended) – pre-trial disclosure

Police Act 1997, Part III (as amended) – interference with property

Regulation of Investigatory Powers Act 2000 (as amended) – covert surveillance

Evidence can be given voluntarily to the police through co-operation. With the appropriate legal authority, it can be obtained by coercive (search warrant – judicial authority) or covert (surveillance – senior police officer authority) means. Police custody presents a context of coercion in which the suspect is rendered particularly amenable to the investigative process (photographs, fingerprints, DNA samples – senior police officer authority). The power to use coercive and covert means to obtain evidence is balanced (how successfully is a matter of legal and civil liberties debate) by the requirement placed on the police to document their processes and reasoning – an obligation intended to achieve transparency of police action and therefore accountability but seen by some investigators as an obstructive bureaucratic burden.

It is a common defence tactic at trial to attack the integrity of police procedure, particularly if the evidence itself is strong or, in the case of surveillance evidence, incontrovertible. Much of the modern law on criminal evidential procedure has arisen from miscarriages of justice and improper police investigation methods.

Reliability

Each form of evidence gathering requires its own specialist skills to ensure the evidence is reliable. Interviewing witnesses to take statements is as much a skill, for instance, as examining a crime scene for finger-prints or a computer hard drive for digital evidence. Investigator training is therefore of paramount importance.

Of particular concern are vulnerable witnesses – children, rape victims, mentally-impaired persons – whose vulnerability (and unwitting unreliability) dictates both special interviewing procedures and special testimony procedures.

Human memory is fallible so witness testimony, although the preferred form of testimony, is not guaranteed to be wholly reliable. Increasingly, expert witness testimony is being called into question. Much publicity surrounds the use of expert witnesses in child abuse cases but two recent miscarriages of justice in Scotland have illustrated how fingerprint identification – relied upon as scientific, ultimate proof for over a hundred years – is in fact no more than expert opinion, and in an adversarial trial system, juries are often confronted by conflicting expert testimony.

Resources

The resourcing issues of evidence gathering are often underestimated. There are more ways to obtain evidence than ever before, partly because so much of an individual's life is documented daily (e.g. by CCTV, by the use of debit and credit cards, by internet and telephone billing).

A shop-lifting investigation may only involve a statement of complaint and one or two witness statements, upon which the suspect will be interviewed and, if appropriate, charged. At the other end of the scale, a murder enquiry will involve the gathering of significant amounts of evidence, which will require computer-assisted analysis and collation (hence the creation of HOLMES as discussed in section 2.10).

It is essential to identify potential witnesses and evidence as soon as possible and so large-scale enquiries can quickly swallow up large numbers of staff, with adverse consequences for the staffing of other police activities. Even witness identification can be complicated. Imagine, for instance, investigating officers, who only speak English, conducting house-to-house enquiries in a block of flats in which a largely immigrant population speak between them 50 languages, none of them having English as their first language.

Digital evidence, which is so prevalent these days, presents particular challenges. On the one hand, computers record everything that is done on them, regardless of deletions; on the other hand, simply switching a computer on to examine it will alter the digital evidential record. Hence ACPO has published special guidelines for the examination of computers to ensure that any forensic examination is fully auditable. Translated into paper documents, the contents of one gigabyte of data will take 4.2 persons working years to read, let alone analyse. It is not uncommon for terabytes (1,000 gigabytes) of digital evidence to be seized from any given suspect, which creates significant logistical problems in analysis and disclosure when, under court rules, the prosecution only has 120 days from the date of charge in which to prepare its case – and to disclose sufficient material to enable the defence the opportunity to prepare its case – and bring the case to Crown Court.

Improved scientific techniques have enhanced the value of, and increased the opportunities to obtain, forensic evidence, but scientific techniques are expensive. Tough management decisions may have to be made about which evidence to submit for forensic examination. A mistake could lead either to a miscarriage of justice or a failed prosecution.

"Why is the PACE power to stop and search contentious?"

This requires an outline of how stop and search came to be enacted; the various different stop and search powers that now exist under different Acts; the research that has been conducted into the impact of stop and search on communities and community policing; and understanding of how many stops result in arrests and the different perspectives on interpreting these statistics.

Taking it **FURTHER**

What are the special measures allowed for vulnerable witnesses, and how successful are they? The trial emphasis on personal testimony creates particular issues for vulnerable witnesses. Special measures have been implemented to cater for this while preserving due process protections for defendants.

Textbook guide

KENNEDY H (2004) *Just Law, London: Vintage*
SMITH J (2002) *'Evidence in criminal cases', in McConville M & Wilson G (eds), The Handbook of the Criminal Justice Process, Oxford: Oxford University Press, pp. 183–204*
SPENCER J (2002) *'Evidence', in Delmas-Marty M & Spencer J (eds), European Criminal Procedures, Cambridge: Cambridge University Press, pp. 594–640*
ZANDER M (2005) *Police and Criminal Evidence Act 1984 (5th edn), London: Sweet & Maxwell*

2.12

policing different types of crime

Core areas: **Strategic options**

Changing trends and techniques

Institutional responses

Practicalities of detection and prevention

Running themes

In varying respects all the following perspectives must be considered in relation to this topic, because different types of crime make different demands and have different consequences and implications for **police organisation**, and **police officers and staff**. How the police manage and respond to different types of crime will have different implications for **the wider community**, and for the handling of **victims, suspects, witnesses** and **third parties**. The need to engage with **other agencies** will vary by crime type, and although the overall impact of crime and crime statistics is a **political issue**, individual crime types also have their own political significance.

Different types of crime make different demands on the police service. But common to all types are four key areas of study:
What strategic/tactical options are available with which to police crime?
Evidential issues
Skills and resources for specialist evidence gathering
Police responses to changing social attitudes towards crime

Strategic options

Along with their peace preservation function, the police are the primary state agents in the investigation of crime (although specific crimes are also investigated by other agencies such as HMRC and HMIS). Policing crime is far from a precise science. For instance, it is estimated that crimes reported to the police and crimes reported during victim surveys significantly underrepresent total criminality. That which is unknown cannot be effectively policed and strategies for detection, deterrence, disruption or diversion can only be formulated on what is known or can reasonably be inferred. The picture is never complete. The strategic options in policing crime generically divide into detection, prevention or regulation.

Detection requires investigation to secure the evidence with which to prosecute offenders and will usually involve the use of police coercive powers.

Prevention sub-divides into a number of tactical options, which do not necessarily dictate police involvement but may rely on partnership between police and other agencies. These options are:

- deterring offenders
- target-hardening (increased physical security)
- diverting potential victims from risk
- disrupting/dismantling criminal markets or organisations

To these can be added *regulation*, for example business and financial regulations designed to prevent fraud and money laundering or counterfeiting, which is 'policed' by non-police agencies such as the Financial Services Authority or Trading Standards Authorities.

Changing trends and techniques

Victorian values (local control of policing, a focus on property offences, the use of public order policing to reinforce socio-economic structures) influenced the framework for policing provision: local forces with defined territorial jurisdiction and an emphasis on preserving the peace as well as detecting reported crimes. This framework has not significantly changed since its inception. But what has changed, in part due to changing social attitudes, is the range of criminal behaviours the police are now expected to deal with.

For example, domestic violence and sexual exploitation of children, both predominantly behaviours that take place away from the public eye, were largely unrecognised as policing issues until the late twentieth century. Now understood for the harm they cause, these behaviours have to be policed through either detection or prevention. In terms of prosecution, the vast majority of these offences have to be brought to trial without third-party eye-witnesses, depending instead upon the testimony of traumatised victims whose vulnerability can be exploited in cross-examination to create reasonable doubt in jurors' minds. Although they should not, acquittals inevitably cast doubt on the victim's version of events, eroding their confidence in the criminal justice system and leaving them potentially vulnerable to further abuse.

The tactical response to this has been the development of sophisticated victim interviewing techniques and special provisions for testifying at trial.

In terms of policing such behaviours through prevention, much more needs to be understood about *victimisation, offender psychology* and *risk management*. Although the police service contributes to such understanding, preventative work with (potential) offenders and (potential) victims will primarily fall to non-police partner agencies.

There have been adverse consequences to increased public awareness about non-visible criminality. In July 2000 the *News of World* conducted a name-and-shame campaign against men it asserted to be paedophiles. Far from enhancing public safety, this campaign prompted vigilantism, thus creating more victims (and more policing problems to be solved) through violent public protests and attacks against those who had been named – in a number of cases quite wrongly. This illustrates the power of the press and public outrage in determining, wittingly or unwittingly, the policing agenda.

Institutional responses

Different crime types have also prompted different responses at an institutional level. Some of these will be considered in more detail below (sections 2.13 to 2.15).

The twentieth-century criminalisation of narcotics created a criminal market economy outside the Victorian experience and policing framework. The creation of specialist police squads was one structural response to policing the drugs problem. In terms of detection, the policing issues are multi-tiered. Local forces are not structured to address cross-border trafficking and therefore must concentrate on dealing both with the drugs market within their police area and the consequential symptoms, such as acquisitive crime, that supports drug-user dependency.

Hate crime, particularly racially motivated crime, has added another dimension to the issues of detection and prevention: police culture.

The institutional consequences of the Macpherson Inquiry are discussed in detail below (Section 2.19). It highlighted how organisational culture can influence policing responses to certain crimes or aspects of crime, and in an ever more cosmopolitan community, this added dimension to any given policing strategy demands ever more sophisticated solutions. Neither detection nor prevention strategies will be fully effective without community support and engagement in such issues. But at the same time as recognising the fundamental truth underpinning the political sound-bite about tackling crime and the causes of crime, appropriate community engagement will of itself create new solution options.

In the various tactical options comprising prevention strategy, the police have a variety of roles to play. The extent to which conviction and punishment deter offending or recidivism is a key criminological debate. The public, in successive opinion polls, repeatedly emphasise the desire for more uniform police foot patrols, regardless of the evidence that such tactics make a minimal contribution to detections and an unproven contribution to crime prevention. From the public perspective, greatest store is set by the reassurance inherent in such patrols. The institutional response has been the extension of the police family to include street wardens and PCSOs, satisfying the reassurance issues without expending expensively trained officers on an activity that draws upon few of their costly skills.

Practicalities of detection and prevention

Prosecution requires evidence. Evidential opportunities and techniques differ by crime type. Also different are the skills required to investigate the evidence. The specialist forensic skills of the 'scenes of crime' investigator are an obvious example. Significant specialist skill is also required in the interviewing of rape victims and other vulnerable victims/witnesses; in the examination of digital data; in the tracing of laundered funds and recovery of criminal assets.

There is thus a significant training demand to be met. Skill is required both in securing the evidence *and* in presenting it at court. Any investigator who betrays an absence of professionalism will undermine the prosecution case by casting doubt over the competence with which the evidence was gathered and, by implication, doubt over the integrity of that evidence.

For the police service this means that the concept of the omni-competent officer, skilled sufficiently to undertake any criminal enquiry, is not sustainable. Specialists are required and specialists inevitably detract from the numbers of staff available to be deployed on other policing activity.

Whatever the crime, the first hour of the investigation (particularly in the case of a recently committed crime) – the 'Golden Hour' – is crucial in terms of evidential opportunity. Mistakes made at this stage, for instance cross-contamination of forensic evidence if victim and suspect are present or proximate, cannot later be corrected. Investigation management is thus as much a necessary skill as specialisms in evidence gathering.

Preventative patrol has already been considered above. The police service used to offer crime prevention advice in relation to target-hardening (better locks, burglar alarms, etc.), but this welfare function of the police is a luxury few forces can now afford unless the role is civil-ianised. Diverting potential victims from risk necessitates public aware-ness campaigns and designing public spaces to minimise crime opportunities (graffiti-resistant paint, thoroughfares devoid of places for muggers to hide, etc.).

"Do crime investigators have to be police officers?"

This invites consideration of the differences between *detection* and *enforcement*. Factors for consideration include the following: the Police Reform Act 2002 creates the role of non-police investigators within police forces; Surrey police use non-police statement-takers; non-police agencies investigate different types of criminal offence; some police forces hire private companies to secure evidence to support ASBO applications.

 Taking it **FURTHER**

Investigation management skills have become as significant as detective skills. What have been the driving forces in developing investigation manage-ment? (Yorkshire Ripper enquiry, miscarriages of justice, NIM).

Textbook guide

FINDLAY M (1999) *The Globalisation of Crime,* Cambridge: Cambridge University Press

GILLING D (1997) *Crime Prevention: Theory, Policy and Politics,* London: UCL Press

GREGORY G & LEES S (1999) *Policing Sexual Assault,* London: Routledge

HAMLYN B ET AL. (2004) *Are Special Measures Working? Evidence from Surveys of Vulnerable and Intimidated Witnesses,* London: Home Office

HOME OFFICE (2003) *Respect and Responsibility – Taking a Stand against Anti-Social Behaviour, Cm 5778,* London: HMSO.

INNES M (2003) *Investigating Murder: Detective Work and the Police Response to Criminal Homicide,* Oxford: Oxford University Press

MAGUIRE M ET AL. (EDS) (2002) *The Oxford Handbook of Criminology,* Oxford: Oxford University Press

2.13	
policing organised crime	

Core areas: **UK institutional responses**

International responses

> *'Organised crime' describes a criminal business methodology, not a criminal offence. It transcends traditional policing geographical and jurisdictional frameworks. It often necessitates international collaboration, the framework for which is determined by diplomatic issues as much as by policing priorities.*

Running themes

With the above in mind, what are the implications and issues to be considered when reflecting upon **police organisation**, **suspects' perspectives**, the concerns of **the wider community** (legitimate or misconceived), the needs of **other agencies**, and **political policy-making**?

'Organised crime' is not a specific offence defined in statute. Rather it is a conceptual model of criminal activity upon which key political strategies are determined that depart from the UK norm of policing that is locally controlled and locally delivered. The political significance of policing organised crime engages international relations as well as domestic politics, and increasingly transnational organised crime is asserted to be a threat to national security (particularly in states that are politically/economically unstable) and to have links with terrorism. Such assertions are used to reinforce arguments favouring exceptional policing measures as a response to organised crime, including special laws and investigative powers.

There is no universally agreed definition but defining characteristics upon which there is some consensus include the following elements identified by the House of Commons Home Affairs Select Committee (1995, p. x):

> Organized crime is distinguishable from other kinds of crime by a number of special features ... [including] the following elements:
>
> – it is a group activity;
> – undertaken for profit;
> – involving long-term criminal activity;
> – frequently international in nature;
> – large scale;
> – frequently combining both licit and illicit operations;
> – involving some form of internal discipline amongst the group, including use of violence and intimidation.

It can encompass either individual criminal organisations or the market/network relationship existing between two or more organisations and generally involves trafficking illicit commodities (drugs, illegal immigrants, arms, counterfeit products) or the provision of illicit services (money-laundering, realisation of criminal profits, unlawful disposal of waste). A local police force might reasonably be expected to address local manifestations of organised crime – street-level drug-dealing or prostitution, for instance – but cannot reasonably be expected to intervene at other points in the supply chain, such as transcontinental human-trafficking, drugs importation, or production in source countries.

UK institutional responses

In 1964 crimes conducted on a scale that transcended force boundaries were recognised as a problem outside the local police framework. Nine

Regional Crime Squads (RCS) were established. These were collaborative efforts resourced by the secondment of officers from the forces in each region. Subsequently reduced to six in number, the RCS suffered from the absence of strategic executive control. This lacuna was addressed in 1998 with the creation of the National Crime Squad (NCS), the first national operational police agency in England and Wales. (Scotland had its own crime squad and Scottish Drugs Enforcement Agency while in Northern Ireland the RUC had responsibility for both organised crime and local policing.)

The six RCS merged into the NCS, headed by a Director-General with chief constable status and powers. A sister agency, originally a Home Office unit, the National Criminal Intelligence Service (NCIS) was reconstituted as a UK-wide non-investigative agency at the same time (Police Act 1997, Parts I and II).

Other agencies also investigated organised crime, for instance HMCE and HMIS in relation to drugs importation and illegal immigration. Collaboration between these different agencies, particularly HMCE and the RCS, was problematic, exacerbated by government performance indicators that brought the agencies into direct competition with each other.

The constitutional arrangements for the NCS and NCIS originally mirrored those for local policing, but this model enjoyed little support and both national agencies became directly funded, non-departmental public bodies in 2001.

A 2004 White Paper outlined significant rethinking about the UK response to organised crime. Asserting three strategic principles –

- the reduction of criminal profits (asset recovery);
- the disruption of criminal markets and businesses; and
- the increase of risk of prosecution/conviction for major criminals

– the White Paper identified the following critical success factors in a new strategy:

(a) the creation of a new organized crime agency to bring a new clarity of approach, with enhanced capabilities and skills;
(b) a radical improvement in the use of intelligence throughout the system;
(c) strong partnership working with individual police forces and other partners, domestically and internationally, ensuring that best practice is identified and spread and delivering a coordinated approach to security at the frontier;
(d) a drive for more concerted use of existing powers and effective relations between investigators and prosecutors; and
(e) new powers to equip the criminal justice system to defeat the most serious criminals and criminal enterprises. (Home office 2004)

The creation of the Serious Organised Crime Agency (SOCA), a non-police agency with police, customs and immigration powers and close connections with MI5, was a direct response to the disincentives militating against agency collaboration. NCS, NCIS, together with the National Hi-Tech Crime Unit (NHTCU), elements from the old HMCE and HMIS, were merged to form the new agency. It became operational on 1 April 2006. SOCA will deal with national and international organised crime that impacts on the UK. Such a remit is likely to utilise all its resources. Thus the problem left unresolved by SOCA's creation is how to respond to regional organised crime within the UK. In some areas initiatives not dissimilar to the old RCS are being created. The 2005 proposal to merge existing shire forces into regional strategic forces was predicated upon the philosophy that larger organisations are better placed to deal with regional-level organised crime.

The development of government thinking in respect of responses to organised crime is documented in: Home Affairs Committee (1995) Organized Crime, Third Report (HC Session 1994–95, 18–I)
Home Office (2004) One Step Ahead: A 21st Century Strategy to Defeat Organized Crime, Cm 6167, London:THMSO

International responses

International responses relevant to the UK divide into G8 and EU initiatives. That these two primarily economic organisations should be interested in transnational organised crime is evidence of the parasitic relationship between organised crime and legitimate economic market infrastructures.

The G8 established its Lyon Group of law enforcement experts in 1996 and has sub-groups, inter alia, on judicial co-operation and hi-tech crime. Good practice is identified and proposed but implementation of legislative/ policing norms can only be achieved through political influence.

International law enforcement co-operation between EU member states operates within the Justice and Home Affairs (JHA), Third Pillar, of the European project. Common and collaborative action against criminality is sought through a variety of measures, joint action plans and initiatives, including Europol, Eurojust (see section 2.7), the European Police College and the European Chief Police Officers' Task Force.

Elsewhere, the USA uses direct economic sanctions as a means of influencing countries to combat transnational organised crime. Although there are profound philosophical differences between the EU and USA in their approaches to transnational organised crime, there has been considerable transatlantic dialogue on this issue.

International efforts focus on promoting substantive domestic legislation capable of being used against organised crime; enhancing mutual legal assistance and international law enforcement co-operation provisions; and support for more investigative resources in individual states.

" In what ways does SOCA depart from traditional policing of organised crime and what are the potential consequences? "

This invites consideration of the constitution of local policing (tripartite) and the novelty of SOCA (UK-wide remit, no direct connection with local policing). A successful answer will incorporate understanding of the RCS/NCS structures and how SOCA differs from these. The second half requires understanding of the so-called 'Level 2' gap.

Taking it ***FURTHER***

This topic invites various avenues of further study:

- In what ways has the EU influenced UK responses to transnational organised crime?
- Does the threat posed by organised crime justify special laws and investigative powers/techniques?
- How and why do the governance arrangements for SOCA differ from those for local policing? Could not the arrangements in place for the NCS have been preserved?

Textbook guide

EDWARDS A & GILL P (EDS) (2003) *Transnational Organised Crime: The Policy and Politics of the Global Crime Problem, London: Routledge*
FIORENTINI G & PELTZMAN S (1995) *The Economics of Organised Crime, Cambridge: Cambridge University Press*
HOBBS D (1994) *'Professional and organized crime in Britain', in Maguire et al. (eds), The Oxford Handbook of Criminology (1st edn), Oxford: Oxford University Press, pp. 441–68*
LEVI M (2002) *'The organisation of serious crimes', in Maguire et al. (eds), The Oxford Handbook of Criminology (3rd edn), Oxford: Oxford University Press, pp. 878–913*
WILLIAMS P & VLASSIS D (EDS) (2001) *Combating Transnational Crime: Concepts, Activities and Responses, London: Frank Cass*

2.14	
policing cyberspace	

Core areas: **Legislative responses**
Police responses
Evidential issues
Computer crime harm

Cyberspace challenges territorially based models of policing and law enforcement. Computers provide new and sophisticated mechanisms for committing long-established criminal behaviours. They also generate their own issues of practicality for evidence presentation.

Running themes

The virtual reality of cyberspace creates its own issues for **police organisation** (e.g. the need for specialist resources; how can the internet be policed?), **police**

officers and staff (e.g. the ability to recognise digital data volatility and preserve/recover digital evidence), **victims** and **third parties,** who are used without their knowledge to disguise criminal attacks, and for suspects whose criminality is unconfined by the constraints of physical geography. The **political implications** of cybercrime (should the internet be policed and, if so, how?) have yet to make an impact on **the wider community,** to whom cybercrime and its consequences remain largely invisible.

Legislative responses

A key problem in drafting legislation to deal with computer-related offending is that the law ideally should be technology-neutral so as to capture future technological developments without necessitating the continual enacting of new or amended legislation (consider how many technological innovations there have been in computing since 1990 when the Computer Misuse Act was passed).

A second important aspect, given that computer-enabled criminality knows no geographical boundaries, is to ensure that as many states as possible subscribe to international norms in defining computer-related criminality and agreeing investigative powers. When a hacker in the UK can steal electronically funds from a US bank and deposit the stolen funds into a Russian bank, prosecution depends on different national jurisdictions and investigative authorities being able lawfully to co-operate. The Council of Europe has negotiated a Cyber Crime Convention (2001) in which non-European states can participate. International consensus and non-treaty based standards are also negotiated in the G8 hi-tech crime sub-group.

Police responses

The G8 called, in 1997, for enhanced protection and investigative capability in relation to computer-enabled criminality, not least because it was recognised that such criminality had the potential to damage considerably national and international economic activity. At the time, the UK had little effective capability outside a very few specialist units in police forces large enough to be able to resource such luxuries.

The 1997 G8 declaration underpinned a concerted effort by ACPO and other investigative agencies to enhance UK capability and this led directly to the creation of the multi-agency National Hi-Tech Crime Unit (NHTCU) (now subsumed into SOCA) and the funding of enhanced capability in every English and Welsh police force over a three-year period. In this regard, industry and the business community regarded the police service as coming very late to the game and private enterprise had done much to protect itself prior to police capability being enhanced. This was in part due to the absence of computer-related crime from police performance indicators. Prior to the NHTCU, such capability as did exist resided in the London police forces and some provincial fraud units. But even the latter were being scaled down and their staff diverted to activity that was measured by Whitehall.

The conceptual change brought about by the team that created the NHTCU cannot be underestimated. The UK is now an active participant in the G8 co-ordinated international 24/7 emergency response network, which seeks to ensure that digital evidence of a crime can be preserved long enough for formal mutual legal assistance requests to be transmitted in securing it for investigation.

A new phenomenon brought about by the transnational possibilities of computer crime is the additional scope for reporting crime that becomes possible. As will be seen below, significant problems were caused to UK law enforcement by a US Postal Service criminal investigation that coincidentally discovered evidence of widespread criminality in the UK, which then had to be investigated. Similarly, the potential existed for considerable cross-border activity between UK forces, another challenge to meeting geographically specific performance indicators.

Evidential issues

Speed is often of the essence in policing computer-related crime because digital evidence is volatile. Data on a hard drive can be over-written (although it is possible to recover such data up to a point) or manipulated, and vital billing data demonstrating access to the internet or transmission of emails is only held temporarily by service providers. Digital data, with the potential to be incontrovertible, is nevertheless volatile and vulnerable.

A second practical issue for investigators is the sheer volume of digital data and the variety of media on which it can be stored. Digital forensic best evidential practice recognises that any examination of a computer automatically changes the evidence and so working copies of hard drives to be investigated have to be made. The original is then preserved for production at court and the digital copy used to conduct examinations. As hard drive capacity increases exponentially, so forensic imaging and examination become more problematic, particularly given the time scales involved in preparing a case for trial and ensuring proper disclosure to the defence.

Guidance on digital evidence best practice, highlighting the key issues, is available at www.acpo.police.uk/asp/policies/Data/gpg_computer_based_evidence_v3.pdf

Where the data is stored is also of importance because powers to access such evidence will be determined by the prevailing jurisdiction in that location, which will not necessarily be the powers available to the investigators. For example, email transaction data may be stored outside the jurisdiction at the central servers of the service provider. Time-consuming mutual legal assistance measures (see section 2.7) must be employed to secure such data if it is not in the UK. Some service providers based in the USA have reached agreement with UK authorities to recognise the UK-based Data Protection Act notices issued by investigators to access names and addresses of email subscribers who have registered using a UK address, so as to avoid the time and expense of mutual legal assistance.

Computer crime harm

Although the most widespread potential socio-economic harm that can be caused by computer-enabled criminality is the damage it can do through successful attacks against the financial IT infrastructure, or to national security from attacks against government or military systems, the computer crime that has captured popular imagination is that of online paedophile activity. There are two extremes to this activity which raise different policing issues.

Operation Cathedral (1999), a multinational joint operation co-ordinated by the NCS, investigated a sophisticated global network of paedophiles operating their own servers and utilising significant counter-investigation measures, including a manual on how to frustrate police investigations and very strict vetting of new recruits to the network. The requirement for network newcomers to share 10,000 images of children being abused effectively ruled out police infiltration because the police could not lawfully or morally produce or acquire such images to support an undercover operation.

Some twenty states were involved in the investigation, although only 12 took part in the simultaneous and co-ordinated enforcement action that was necessary to ensure that as many of the network as possible were arrested at the same time so that evidence was not lost and participants did not escape. Securing such co-ordinated action across 12 national jurisdictions meant overcoming significant procedural problems in states where the execution of search and arrest warrants is confined to certain times of day.

Operation Cathedral was an investigation into serious, organised criminality; thus the investigation sat naturally (pre-NHTCU) with the NCS.

Operation Ore (2002) caused entirely different problems. US Postal Service investigators set up a website purporting to contain paedophile images and charging users for access. Those who logged on and sought access using their credit cards were then traced via the card number and arrested. The US authorities identified over 7,000 suspects residing in the UK. Their names were passed to NCIS.

As these were individuals committing crime alone, they fell outside the organised crime remit of the new NHTCU. It was also clear that if any of the suspects seeking access to the purported images had access to children, then potentially there was a risk of physical abuse that had to be averted. These factors meant that the onus for following up these 7,000 suspects fell to local forces (rather than the NHTCU), most of whom did not have the capacity to do so with any speed. Suspects were risk assessed and investigated on a priority basis, according to the immediate physical risk they posed to children.

The issues raised by Operation Ore in part led to the creation of yet another specialist unit, the Paedophile Online Investigation Team (POLIT), which metamorphosed into the Child Exploitation Online Protection Centre (CEOPs) in 2006. Unlike US agencies, UK law enforcement does not have the resources available to conduct the sort of proactive operations that led to Operation Ore.

Operation Ore raises moral, practical and legal issues. Should UK authorities be conducting such sting operations? Given that the UK police service struggled to resource Operation Ore, how will the next such operation be managed? Where are the extra resources going to come from? If available computer investigative capacity focuses on paedophile crimes, what risks have to be accepted (and by whom) in relation to other computer-enabled criminality that will go uninvestigated? If chief constables and BCU commanders are measured by their handling of policing within their specific area of responsibility, what is the incentive for police to deal with cross-border computer criminality that could exhaust their resources and divert effort away from areas in which poor performance could result in punitive sanction?

"What obstacles exist to the successful transnational investigation of computer-enabled crime, and what measures have been adopted to overcome the obstacles?"

This two-part question requires an understanding of how computer criminals commit crime exploiting different criminal jurisdictions and knowledge of what measures have been created to ensure successful investigation and prosecution. It is probably best approached by way of a case study. Any given case study will have its own issues and so caution should be exercised when trying to infer generalities.

Taking it *FURTHER*

Clifford Stoll (1989) *The Cuckoo's Egg: Tracking a Spy Through the Maze of Computer Espionage*, New York: Pocket Books, is an excellent account for non-specialists on how to detect a hacking attack.

Textbook guide

BARRETT N (1997) *Digital Crime: Policing the Cybernation*, London: Kogan Page

JEWKES Y (2003) 'Policing cybercrime', in T Newburn (ed.), *Handbook of Policing*, Cullompton: Willan, pp. 501–24

MACVEAN A & SPINDLER P (EDS) (2003) *Policing Paedophiles on the Internet*, London: The New Police Bookshop

SUSSMAN M (1999) 'The critical challenges from international high-tech and computer-related crime at the Millennium', *Duke Journal of Comparative & International Law 9 (2)*, pp. 451–89

WALL D (2001) *Crime and the Internet*, London: Routledge

2.15

policing terrorism

Core areas: **Prevention by making communities and the environment unsafe for the terrorist. Prevention by proactivity, including intelligence-led disruption or preventive detention. Expert emergency response at the scene of a terrorist incident and investigation of the circumstances in the effective collection of evidence for the suceessful prosecution of offenders**

Key thinkers

One community's freedom fighter is another community's terrorist. **Mao Zedong** described the terrorist as a freedom fighter, a fish swimming in the sea of the community.

Running themes

Policing terrorism – and the fear of terrorism – brings its own particular demands on **police organisations**, not least because of the **political implications** and the consequences on **the wider community**, both of a terrorist attack and a government response. In relation to **suspects**, precisely what rights should be protected and how, if at all, are issues being hotly debated since the terrorist bombings in New York, Bali, Madrid and London. Increased constraints on civil liberties in an attempt to frustrate further terrorist attacks effectively makes citizens who were not actually harmed by the original outrage the **victims** of secondary terrorism: the fear and unrest associated with government responses to the threat.

Terrorism is defined in different ways in different countries by different legislation but the core issue is one of achieving political ends by illegal violence or the threat of violence. It is summed up by the mantra: 'Kill ten people terrify ten thousand people, kill a hundred terrorise ten million, kill a thousand terrorise a hundred million.' Over 3,000 people were killed during the course of the 'Troubles' in mainly Northern Ireland but also in

England, Wales, Scotland, Republic of Ireland and elsewhere in Europe between 1968 and 1998. A similar number were killed on one day, 11 September 2000, in the USA. Each terrorist act may also be a crime under other statutes (e.g. grevious bodily harm, murder, criminal damage). The causes or perceived justification may be elsewhere than in the UK. There may be international investigative needs, translation or cultural intricacy.

The police response is part of an overall government strategy that is similar in some ways to responses to other crimes and uses partnerships, other agencies, alliances, and international conventions. But there are also important differences. The consequences of a particular terrorist act may be vastly more damaging than other crimes. For example, the deployment of nuclear, chemical, biological or radioactive threats or devices can cause incomparable fear or injuries, and the police and other emergency services need specialist clothing and equipment.

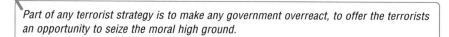

Part of any terrorist strategy is to make any government overreact, to offer the terrorists an opportunity to seize the moral high ground.

Another mantra is 'communities defeat terrorism': the opposite of the Mao Zedong theory that the terrorist is a freedom fighter swimming in the seas of communities, sustained and protected by anonymity in the community. The police task is to make the environment unsafe for them.

The policing response is called 'counter terrorism' and may be analysed as a threefold response:

1. Prevention by making communities and the environment unsafe for the terrorist.

2. Prevention by proactivity, including intelligence-led disruption or preventive detention.

3. Expert emergency response at the scene of a terrorist incident and investigation of the circumstances in the effective collection of evidence for the successful prosecution of offenders.

The unified response of government, police, other agencies, business and communities is sometimes called 'UK Counter Terrorism plc' to indicate the shared strategy and intentions.

Prevention by making communities and the environment unsafe for the terrorist

This has many of the ingredients we have discussed in the policing framework (see particularly sections 2.4 (engaging with the public), 2.5 (philosophies of policing) and also 2.19 (race and diversity)).

On the one hand, this is about police cultivation of personal and group security, the location of CCTV and its effectiveness and maintenance, the emergency evacuation, resilience or protective measures. On the other hand, it is also about denying terrorist groups the security through anonymity they seek to prepare their plans. It is about monitoring materials they may need – garages, safe houses, cars – and raising the threshold of suspicion that will encourage reporting on specialist counter-terrorist hotlines. That is the meaning of 'communities defeat terrorism'. Meanwhile, the terrorists will try to represent such policing measures as oppressive, spying on the community, and an abuse of human rights. The community impact assessment, which identifies the potentially dysfunctional aspects or unintended consequences before any counter-terrorist operation, requires considerable local knowledge and sensitivity. Sometimes because of the potential consequences of a terrorist success, there is not enough time to complete the assessment task.

Prevention by proactivity, including intelligence-led disruption or preventive detention

This has many of the ingredients we have discussed in the policing framework (see particularly intelligence-led policing in section 2.5 on the philosophies of policing). When considering policing activity against terrorists, particularly proactive policing operations, the issue of conflicting human rights predominates. The rights of members of the public and the rights of the terrorists need to be balanced – the right to life under article 2 of the European Convention on Human Rights, for example.

One of the stated intentions of some terrorist groups is to cause the frustrated or horrified members of the security forces, including the police, to overreact, to cause injury or death. Michael Collins, head of intelligence for a precursor group to the Provisional IRA (PIRA) in 1920/21, was quite clear about his intention to goad the security forces into violent behaviour. The police can also mis-identify terrorists, as events at Stockwell on 22 July 2005 illustrate.

When balancing conflicting human rights, the police use an acronym PLAN BI:

- *proportionate*
- *legal*
- *accountable*
- *necessary*
- *acting on the best information available*

Many of these decisions are made in split seconds. The IPCC and Crown Prosecution Service took a year to investigate the Stockwell operation before deciding against the criminal prosecution of participating officers.

Expert emergency response at the scene of a terrorist incident and investigation of the circumstances in the effective collection of evidence for the successful prosecution of offenders

This has many of the ingredients discussed in sections 2.3 and 2.4, where we considered government, other agencies and partnership, and 2.10 on criminal investigations. One difference is the scale and complexity of emergency response policing and a return to normality conducted in parallel with a criminal investigation. There are similarities to the scene of a rail or aircraft disaster.

Two examples illustrate some aspects of these similarities despite differences, and differences despite similarities. First, the crime scene at the South Quay PIRA bomb on 9 February 1996, which ended the PIRA ceasefire, was half a mile in diameter and included a flooded, disused, rubbish-filled dock. The back axle of a lorry that delivered the bomb, an important exhibit, was found on top of a building a quarter of a mile from the epicentre. There were over 300 GBH victims and two murder victims. The criminal damage was valued at £500 million. Secondly, the London bombings on 7 July 2005 caused 49 deaths at three different locations, two deep in the Underground transport system, and over 200 other injuries. There was widespread economic disruption to businesses that had to be managed.

Some of the policing tasks are generic whatever the crime being investigated, such as exhibit handling (though on a massive scale), family liaison with victims and their families, surveillance, and the authorisation of firearms officers. Other tasks are specific, for example the need of explosives officers and disaster victim identification teams.

Because of the causes célèbres terrorist cases that have miscarried in the past (e.g. Guildford Four, Birmingham Six, Judith Ward), the degree of legal and forensic science challenges and the scale of disclosure research that is required for trial, prosecution of terrorist cases are among the most complex and lengthy trials.

Recent legislation relating to policing terrorism in UK

Terrorism Act 2000
Anti-terrorism, Crime and Security Act 2001
Crime (International Co-operation) Act 2003
Prevention of Terrorism Act UK London 2005
Serious Organised Crime and Police Act 2005
Terrorism Act 2006

See also:

Walker C (1992) *The Prevention of Terrorism in British Law* (2nd edn), Manchester: Manchester University Press
Elagab O (1995) *International Law Documents Relating to Terrorism*, London: Cavendish

---

Policing terrorism is a multifaceted task that can involve all the aspects considered here and all the roles that police officers can undertake. Any one of those tasks or roles can come under a spotlight. When the terrorist task is completed, the police have to go on policing. And that can be as complex as the counter-terrorist task, as Mulcahy (2006) and the Northern Ireland Independent Monitoring Commission Reports (2003–06) have shown.

"Does terrorism necessitate a different policing response from other crimes?"

Given that terrorism is a crime in English law, answers should avoid theoretical discussions about political offences and focus on proportionality in relation both to specific investigative powers and policing strategy. Is the policing response merely an issue of resources, or are the police powers applicable to other crimes simply inadequate to investigate/prevent terrorism?

Taking it **FURTHER**

Is terrorism a different kind of crime to all others? How can an effective policing response avoid fulfilling the terrorists' desire for the police to be seen as overreacting in the eyes of some communities?

Ashworth A (2002) *Human Rights, Serious Crime and Criminal Procedure*, London: Sweet & Maxwell (provides an illuminating and readable legal perspective)

May, Sir John (1992) (1994) *Reports of the Inquiry into the circumstances surrounding the convictions arising out of the Bomb Attacks in Guildford and Woolwich in 1974*, London: HMSO (see also the obituaries in the *Times* and *Durham NC Guardian*, 20 January (1997):

Neyroud P & Beckley A (2001) *Policing Ethics and Human Rights*, Cullompton: Willan (will help you explore proportionality and necessity in armed police operations against terrorists from a policing perspective)

O'Hara P (2005) *Why Law Enforcement Agencies Fail: Mapping Organizational Fault Lines in Policing*, Carolina Academic Press (looks at failures in respect of 9/11)

Textbook guide

CARLILE, LORD (2007) *The Definition of Terrorism CM 7052, London: The Stationery Office*

GRISET P & MAHAN S (2003) *Terrorism in Perspective, London: Sage*

HARNDEN T (1999) *'Bandit County': The IRA and South Armagh, London: Hodder & Stoughton*

INDEPENDENT MONITORING COMMISSION NORTHERN IRELAND (2003–2006) *Reports 1–12, London: HMSO.*

MATASSA M & NEWBURN T (2003) *'Policing and terrorism', in T. Newburn (ed.), Handbook of Policing, Cullompton: Willan*

MULCAHY A (2006) *Policing Northern Ireland: Conflict, Legitimacy and Reform, Cullompton: Willan*

TAYLOR P (1993) *States of Terror, London: Penguin*

2.16

private policing

Core areas: **Sheer size**
The relationship between private and state policing
Private policing of public spaces
Gated communities and ghettos
Accountability of private policing

Running themes

The running themes of particular interest in this section involve **police organisations** and their relationship with private policing, how **other agencies** engage with private policing companies (e.g. in the policing of public spaces such as shopping malls), and the relationship between **the wider community** and private policing, which also engages the relationship between the wider community and police organisations in those areas where the community have bought in private policing provision because they are not getting the service they want (usually guaranteed street patrols) from the public police. The **political implications** of increased private policing provision are also of importance. The **statistical data** reveals the great extent of private policing, which far exceeds the public police in terms of numbers employed, and the considerable economic value of the private policing market.

Sheer size

It is important to distinguish between the specifics of the 'police' and 'policing'. The police are an institution while policing is a set of processes with explicit social functions. Policing may be carried out by a diverse arrangement of individuals and organisations. The increasing fragmentation of policing has created powerful private policing arrangements that have assumed a significant role in terms of size and function. While the UK private security market is growing, it still remains smaller than those in the USA, Canada, Australia and South Africa, where the number of security personnel per capita is more than three times greater than Britain.

Calculating the size of the private policing market is problematic due to the lack of official data, but information from the British Security Industry Association (BSIA) estimated that in 2004 approximately 600,000 people work in the UK security industry, which has a turnover of £5.15 billion. This compared to just over 140,000 police officers, 4,599 community support officers and 12,500 Special Constables (as of February 2005). In addition, the number of BSIA member security-guarding companies employed 75,500 security officers in 2005 with a turnover of £1.575 billion. The significant increase in physical security-guarding has been matched by technology security, with over 4.25 million CCTV cameras installed in the UK and the security system sector having a turnover of £654 million (in 2005).

It has been estimated that there are over 8,000 security companies in the UK, although it is important to note that many of these are small in size and are not members of the BSIA. However, reflecting the size of the market, there are also many multinational companies, such as Group4, which employs over 400,000 full- and part-time personnel worldwide.

Like the police, private policing companies provide a variety of functions which can be divided into three sections: staffed services, security equipment and investigation.

The relationship between private and state policing

The Patten Report (1999) raised the issue of how best police officers can adapt to a world in which their own efforts are only a part of the overall policing in society. In addition, the Police Reform Act (2002) aimed to create a wider 'police family' which embraced the strengths of the private sector. These included the ability to work with and provide bespoke services to the public sector with responsibilities relating to crime, thus freeing up the police and other agents to focus on their core duties. Such functions include court warrant services, court security and custody assistance, lost/found/seized property management, scene of crimes protection, town centre CCTV, statement taking, street and warden patrols.

The developing relationship has seen a mutual collaboration and exchange of techniques, practices and attitudes. The state police has particularly benefited from the technological equipment and skills that the private sector offered, while the private police has adopted the symbolic powers and image through the wearing of uniforms and espousing certain behaviours.

Crawford (2003) has identified four different types of relationship:

- *Integrationist – forms of policing are integrated within the immediate police family, such as PCSOs.*
- *Steering – where the state police seek to govern at a distance the policing activities of others, such as traffic wardens and accredited community safety officers.*
- *Networked – whereby plural policing providers link together in local security provision, such as the partnership arrangement directed under the Crime and Disorder Act (1998).*
- *Market model – where competition determines the relationships between private and state policing in the provision of services.*

Private policing of public spaces

Shearing and Stenning (1981) have argued that the changes in land use and property industry have given rise to corresponding changes in policing, particularly to facilities that are privately owned but to which the public have access and use. These would include shopping malls, hospitals, leisure and entertainment centres. Such developments have provided private commercial organisations with the incentive to define and organise their own policing requirements. This has produced a new form of policing that is characterised by the creation of 'safe space'. Thus the emphasis is more proactive than reactive, focusing on loss prevention and risk reduction rather than law enforcement. Consensual forms of control and regulation are enforced through removal, dismissal and exclusion strategies rather than coercive methods. People's behaviour is regulated by membership and access, ensuring that the appearance of a safe environment is not compromised. Policing public spaces utilises a range of tools, including physical and technological systems such as security guards and CCTV.

The Human Rights Act applies only to public authorities and sub-contractors working for public authorities. Therefore private security/policing is not subject to the HRA unless working on behalf of a public authority.

Gated communities and ghettos

The development of gated communities has been slower in the UK than the USA. Gated communities restrict public access and are often policed using CCTV and security guards, and residents enter into a contractual agreement to regulate their conduct. In the USA it is estimated that 11% of all new housing and over 4 million people live in walled and gated communities, some the size of small towns and exhibiting all the policing problems of towns. The segregation and seclusion approach of gated communities has reconfigured community and neighbourhood relations in terms of policing.

While some members of the population are able to pay for private policing, others are not. The state policing of residential areas has been directed by the political agenda for law and order, which advocates being 'tough on crime' through enforcing measures such as anti-social behaviour orders (ASBOs) and the 'three strikes and you're out' policy. The policing of residential areas has been extended to a range of agencies, including crime and disorder partnerships, housing associations and environmental health officers. Control and compliance is ensured through a range of civil and administrative powers that can exclude residents from the area or evict them from their properties. These powers have been strengthened through legislation such as the Housing Act 1996. These forms of policing have been described as intrusive, with residents claiming that they are 'over policed and under protected'.

Accountability of private policing

However, despite the close partnership between the private and state police, it still largely remains the responsibility of the state police to construct cases for prosecution. In many cases the commercial objectives of private security are often incompatible with legal process. This lack of legal oversight indicates a potential for accountability and malpractice. The government has adopted a non-intervention position in regulating private security, allowing it to develop largely unchecked. Accountability is often implemented through contractual arrangements and obligations. The Private Security Industry Act 2001 required the Security Industry Authority (SIA) to 'establish a voluntary system of inspection of providers of security services, under which those which satisfactorily meet the agreed standards may be registered as approved, and may advertise themselves as such'. The Act does not specify the exact nature of the approval scheme nor how it should operate but sought to professionalise and co-ordinate the private sector.

❝ To whom, if anyone, is private policing accountable? ❞

This requires an understanding of why policing needs to be accountable and invites consideration of accountability mechanisms for the public police (e.g. police authorities) and comparison with accountability in the private sector (e.g. shareholders, and any regulatory bodies overseeing aspects of private policing).

Taking it **FURTHER**

Evidence has shown that motivations for living in a gated community are primarily driven by a perceived need for security and a more generalised fear of crime. Importantly, there was no apparent desire to come into contact with the 'community' within the gated or walled area. What are the implications for community policing and the reassurance agenda?

Atkinson R and Flint J (2004) 'Fortress UK? Gated communities, the spatial revolt and of the elites and time–space trajectories of segregation', *Housing Studies* 19 (6), pp. 875–92

Textbook guide

BUTTON M (2002) *Private Policing, Cullompton: Willan*
HOBBS D ET AL. (2003) *Bouncers: Violence and Governance in the Night-time Economy, Oxford: Oxford University Press*
JOHNSON L (1992) *The Rebirth of Private Policing, London: Routledge*
JONES T & NEWBURN T (1998) *Private Security and Public Policing, Oxford: Oxford University Press*

the cultural context of policing	

2.17	
police ethics and human rights	

Of all the elements of the criminal justice system (pre-trial, trial and post-trial), the police service is perhaps the most exposed in terms of direct interaction with the public, not least because, as the gateway to the criminal justice system, the police exercise considerable discretion in determining who is made subject of that system. Many more people encounter the police than a jury or a magistrate, let alone a prison or probation officer. This has led to an increasing focus upon police behaviour as society continues the unending task of balancing individual and community rights when securing and reconciling human rights.

Neyroud and Beckley (2001, p.4) argue that focusing on ethics and human rights provides the way forward 'out of the cycle of "boom" (such as crime-fighting, zero tolerance, and proactive policing) and "bust" (corruption, miscarriages of justice and scandal) which have characterised recent policing history [*sic*]'.

Running themes

In this subject area different perspectives are clearly pitted against each other. For example, and as will be discussed below, **victims** and **suspects** have conflicting interests. The rights of individuals must be balanced against what is fair and appropriate in the interests of **the wider community**. The actions and attitudes of **police organisations**, their **police officers and staff** must be characterised by integrity, independence and impartiality. This applies not only to police dealings with individuals but also in their dealings with **other agencies** and **third parties** who are neither victims, suspects nor **witnesses**. At a time when the state is accruing to itself ever more draconian powers, justifying such developments with the need to protect society from terrorist attack, the **political focus** on rights and ethics has never been sharper. When each case has to be determined on its merits, what value are general **statistics** in such a debate? If they show a pattern of disproportionate action (excessive use of stop and search on particular ethnic minorities, for instance), then unethical behaviour and attitudes may be the root cause. Equally, the political focus on performance measurement, itself intended to provide greater transparency, may actually encourage unethical behaviour through the necessity of meeting targets.

Significant episodes in highlighting poor policing standards	
1969	*The Times* exposes organisational culture in New Scotland Yard
1974	The Birmingham Six, Guildford Four and Judith Ward – all miscarriages of justice brought about by a desire to secure a conviction
1976	*R v Turnbull* sets criteria for evaluating quality of identification evidence
1980–82	*Operation Countryman*: an investigation into MPS corruption
1989	Corruption in West Midlands Serious Crime Squad exposed
1999	Stephen Lawrence Inquiry identifies unwitting institutional racism

Key thinkers

Geoffrey Robertson QC has written what is widely regarded as the leading text on liberties in the UK: *Freedom, the Individual and the Law* (7th edn), London: Penguin, 1993
Peter Neyroud, Chief Executive of the National Police Improvement Agency, and **Alan Beckley,** Head of Management Development Training, West Mercia Constabulary, have written a useful text on these subjects: *Policing, Ethics and Human Rights*, Cullompton: Willan, 2001

Defining Police Ethics

Human rights law, which is intended to protect individual citizens from the abuse or misuse of state power, provides a formal protection framework articulated in international instruments, domestic statute (the Human Rights Act 1998 [HRA]) and case law. The concept of *police ethics* has no such formal expression. No official statement of ethics has been adopted by the British police service and there are different philosophies of ethics. The overriding objective is to ensure that the police do the right things in the right way for the right reasons.

Such an aspiration can be deceptively simple. For instance, the promotion of performance management by the Thatcher and Blair governments seems superficially to offer a transparent measure to ensure that the police are doing the right things for the right reasons. But the imposition of performance targets injects another permutation into the number of influences that *may* induce or tempt unethical behaviour – as police managers, their future careers dependent upon performance, struggle to meet the targets rather than necessarily do what needs to be done.

In his summary of the literature on police ethics, Neyroud (2003), identifies four themes when considering ethical policing:

- Professionalism
- Use of discretion
- Covert policing
- Corruption

That which is *unethical* is relatively easy to recognise (e.g. failing to meet professional standards, over-reaching discretion, non-compliance with the HRA or relevant legislation such as RIPA, or acting corruptly by taking bribes). Philosophers have, however, struggled to define what is *ethical*.

Finding no substantive aid in the dichotomy of the 'ethics of duty' versus the 'ethics of utility' (otherwise termed the right *means* versus the right *ends*), or in the 'ethics of virtue' or the 'ethics of care', Neyroud hypothesises an alternative approach based on prima facie principle applied in a practical way in which the issue of *proportionality* is key.

Proportionality is a human rights law test that determines whether it is right and proper, under the circumstances, for state authorities to act in a particular way. Just because state authorities have the capability and capacity does not necessarily justify utilisation. For instance, it may well be appropriate to deploy intrusive surveillance techniques (telephone taps or bugged conversations) against terrorists and organised crime gangs, but it would be disproportionate to use such techniques against shop-lifters, against whom less intrusive surveillance by store detectives and CCTV is appropriate. It equally applies in the use of force by police officers, which operates along a continuum ranging from verbal communication (requesting or directing the cessation of offensive behaviour yet causing no harm to the offender), to taking hold of a suspect's arm when arresting that person, to using pepper spray in order to prevent or deflect a personal attack, on to the use of batons as a defence (which is likely to cause injury) and finally to the use of firearms (in which loss of life is a significant risk). Proportionality applied to the force continuum dictates that firearms will not be used where any less lethal intervention will achieve satisfactory resolution.

In case law terms, proportionality is defined by a number of key tests established at the European Court of Human Rights in Strasbourg.

Proportionality key points

1   Have relevant and sufficient reasons based on reliable information been put forward for conducting the proposed (covert) investigation in that particular way? *Jersild v Denmark* [1995] 19 *European Human Rights Reports* [EHRR] 1.

2   Could the same evidence or intelligence [or evidence] be gained by a less intrusive method? *Campbell v UK* [1993] 15 EHRR 137.

3   Is the decision-making process by which the application is made and the authorisation given, demonstrably fair? *W v UK* [1988] 10 EHRR 29, *McMichael v UK* [1995] 20 EHRR 205, *Buckley v UK* [1997] 23 EHRR 101.

4   What safeguards have been put in place to prevent abuse of the technique [or power]? *Klass v Germany* [1978] 2 EHRR 214. See para 59 in which it is argued safeguards represent the compromise between defending democratic society and individual rights.

5   Does the proposed infringement in fact destroy the 'very essence' of the ECHR right engaged?

Based on K Starmer (1999), *European Rights Law*, London: Legal Action Group, pp. 171, 175–6.

Human Rights Law

If ethical behaviour is difficult to define precisely – ACPO have not exhibited any lead on the issue and have failed to adopt any formal position on the issue – then human rights law is, in a sense, less problematic because of the statutory obligation. The HRA 1998 makes it unlawful for a public authority (or sub-contractors employed by and acting on behalf of such an authority) to act in a way that is incompatible with the ECHR (s. 6 HRA).

Articles in Part I of the European *Convention on Human Rights and Fundamental Freedoms*, 1950 (those in bold are of particular relevance to policing).

1   Obligation to respect human rights
2   **Right to life**
3   **Prohibition of torture**
4   Prohibition of slavery and forced labour
5   **Right to liberty and security**
6   **Right to a fair trial**
7   **No punishment without law**
8   **Right to respect for private and family life**
9   Freedom of thought, conscience and religion
10   Freedom of expression
11   **Freedom of assembly**
12   Right to marry
13   **Right to have effective remedy**
14   **Prohibition of discrimination**
15   Derogation on time of emergency [the UK has derogated from Art. 5 for terrorist matters]
16   Restrictions on political activity of aliens
17   Prohibition of abuse of rights
18   Limitation on use of restriction on rights

Parts II and III deal with the procedures of the Strasbourg Court and miscellaneous provisions

Protocol I, 1952, Protection of property
Protocol 6, 1983, Abolition of death penalty

The full text and further information are accessible at www.echr.info. Reading the full text of each article is crucial to understanding its significance (see also Starmer 1999).

The statutory framework imposes clear obligations on police organisations, their officers and staff, and provides the public with a mechanism for redress in the event that state agencies fail to comply with the HRA. It is not a positive statement, the purpose of which is to promote ethics; rather the statutory framework is a means of constraining the behaviour of the state and its agents in order to inhibit actions that would constitute unethical behaviour. Thus human rights law is related to, but is also distinct from, police ethics.

External oversight

It can be argued that there are other possible interventions which can be implemented to promote ethical behaviour through public participation in or oversight of policing activity. Within the context of the custody suite, for instance, doctors, lawyers and independent custody visitors (who used to be called lay visitors: volunteers from the community who are appointed to make unannounced inspections of custody suites to scrutinise treatment of detainees and the conditions in which they are held) each provide a means of independent oversight of police behaviour. In the wider community, Independent Advisory Groups have been established to advise police on issues and operations likely to touch upon particular community sensitivities. These mechanisms for lay oversight of the police are intended to promote ethical considerations and behaviour and can be a means of disclosing unethical behaviour.

Common pitfall: *Article 8 is not a right to privacy and a private life, but a right to respect for private and family life. It is therefore qualified and provided there is statutory provision to do so (e.g. RIPA), its protections may be breached in certain circumstances, such as intrusive surveillance for serious crime.*

Absolute rights *are rights that cannot be breached (e.g. the right to life).*
Qualified rights *are those that may be breached if domestic law allows (e.g. the right to respect of private and family life). Policing itself would breach this right were it not for the statutory provisions of PACE, RIPA and other laws giving the police specific powers.*

Victims' rights

Regular contact often, and unsurprisingly, leaves police officers and staff feeling sympathetic towards victims. However, it would be unethical for police to side with victims. Human rights and victim rights are often and easily confused. The box below explains the distinction. It is the job of the police to be impartial, to represent not the vested interest of victims (despite the fact that the police have more contact with victims than any other state agency), but the wider public interest vested in the state. This highlights different interpretations of 'justice'. For a victim, 'justice' might mean restitution or even vengeance. For the state, it means the impartial and independent examination of the facts, consideration of which then informs state action (e.g. sentencing an accused defendant who is found guilty at trial).

VICTIMS' RIGHTS AND HUMAN RIGHTS LAW

There has been much public comment arguing that the HRA protects the rights of suspects but not victims. This has led to political calls to redress the balance of the criminal justice system in favour of victims. Such perceptions betray a fundamental misunderstanding about human rights law, or perhaps a cynical play upon popular misconceptions for the purposes of political advantage. The HRA protects individual citizens from the abuse of state power. Those who suffer crime are victims of the behaviour of another individual, not the state. Their redress is through the criminal law (and also potentially the civil law), not human rights law.

Kennedy makes a cogent case for a dispassionate criminal justice system, free from undue victim influence (2004, pp. 13, 24 and 210). Garner's journalistic account (2004) of a notorious Australian murder trial from the perspective of the victim's family (who are also victims, of course) juxtaposes the emotional needs and 'common sense justice' from the victims' perspective with the dispassionate perspective a judge has to take. Ashworth (2002, pp. 10–11) makes the point that the criminal process and sentencing are carried out independently and impartially in the wider public interest. The victim is represented as part of the wider public but can never be impartial or independent.

Suspects are not afforded greater rights than victims. They are entitled to different rights because, unlike victims, suspects are particularly vulnerable in their asymmetrical power relationship with the state. The litany of miscarriages of justice illustrates this only too clearly.

Neyroud and Beckley (2001) drew upon the related, but not identical, traditions of *ethics philosophy* and *human rights law* when proposing the following seven principles as a foundation for ethical policing (summarised in Neyroud 2003, p. 584). Adherence to this principled foundation, they argue, will help ensure that the police do the right things for the right reasons and thus police in an ethical manner.

Respect for personal autonomy – derived from the ethics of duty, respecting individuals' rights, treating the public and colleagues with dignity and respect, not using either as a means to an end

Beneficence and non-malificence – police officers helping people without harming others

Justice – respect for human rights and for morally respectable laws

Responsibility – requiring officers to justify their actions

Care – emphasising the interdependence of police, individuals and the community

Honesty – a key virtue central to the legitimacy and authority of policing

Stewardship – emphasising trusteeship over the powerless and over police powers

---

" How has the Human Rights Act influenced police operational decision-making? "

The key to this question lies in justifiable action and accountable decisions. Structuring an answer around the PLAN BI acronym discussed in section 2.15 is one possible approach.

" What gets measured, gets done. What ethical dangers are inherent in the performance agenda? "

Examiners will expect to see discussion of how performance priorities are set and whether or not this agenda-setting takes into consideration the running theme perspectives identified above. It might be useful to employ a case study: if there are no performance targets in relation to vice and prostitution in a police area, it is likely that police resources will be devoted to crimes and anti-social behaviour (including detection and prevention) that is audited. Yet what are the ethical issues arising from such resource allocation when women in the sex industry are generally victims and the wider community can be considered to suffer secondary victimisation in areas where street prostitution occurs.

Taking it *FURTHER*

The extent to which the post-9/11 so-called 'war on terror' justifies retreating from human rights standards is the key debate at the start of the twenty-first century. Is it right to detain persons indefinitely without charge and without presenting evidence at trial? Is it right to act upon or admit as evidence information obtained by torture? The reader is once again directed towards Helena Kennedy (2004) *Just Law: The Changing face of Justice and Why it Matters To Us All*, London: Vintage, as a starting point for further consideration.

Textbook guide

ASHWORTH A (2002) *Human Rights, Serious Crime and Criminal Procedure*, London: Sweet & Maxwell

GARNER H (2004) *Joe Cinque's Consolation: A True Story of Death, Grief and the Law*, Sydney: Picador

KENNEDY H (2004) *Just Law: The Changing Face of Justice and Why It Matters To Us All*, London: Vintage

NEWBURN T (ED.) (2005) *Policing: Key Readings*, Cullompton: Willan, five papers in Part E.

NEYROUD P (2003) 'Policing and ethics', in T Newburn (ed.), *Handbook of Policing*, Cullompton: Willan, pp. 578–602

STARMER K (1999) *European Human Rights Law*, London: Legal Action Group

2.18

the organisational culture of the police

An organisational culture is defined as the deeper level of assumptions and beliefs that are shared by members of an organisation, that operates and projects unconsciously an organisation's view of itself and environment. All organisations have cultures, but the police are a unique organisation because officers are empowered to enforce the law. The importance of these powers is that although the police can invoke the law, they have discretion not to do so if an alternative resolution is appropriate. Hence law in action is characterised by the exercising of discretion. Discretionary choices are influenced and informed by a culture of practice that has developed within the police culture and is arguably difficult to control. Although discretion is associated with negative connotations, Lord Scarman positively described it in his report on the Brixton riots as the art of suiting action to particular circumstances, as the better part of police valour (1981: paragraphs 5.41–5.42 and 7.2–2.6). However, one of the problems with discretion is not that it exists, but how it is exercised. Some groups or members of the community are more likely to be disadvantaged by the exercise of police powers and discretion than others.

Running themes

The following both influence and are informed by (police) organisational culture: **police organisational** perspectives; the perspectives and actions of **police officers and staff**; **victims**' experiences at the hands of the criminal and the police; **suspect** perspectives; **third-party** perspectives; **witness** perspectives; **other agency** perspectives; the experience of **the wider community,** which in turn determines levels of support for and trust in the police; and **political perspectives**.

The focus of police discretion and law in action has been directed at the rank and file where it manifests at street level. This culture if often referred to as the cop or canteen culture of the police.

Cop culture has been defined as a developed pattern of understandings and behaviour that help officers cope with and adjust to the pressures and tensions confronting the police (Reiner 2000, p. 87).

The following characteristics have been identified in 'cop culture' (based on Reiner 2000).

Mission – Action – Cynicism – Pessimism

- *Mission – Policing is perceived by the police as a mission, not just a job but a way of life. The police protect the weak and helpless against the predatory villains and preserve a valued way of life. In doing so the police regard policing as a game of wit and skill in the oppression of law breakers.*
- *Action – Policing is a positive world of action that is symbolised by the 'chase'. This chase is often referred to as 'twos and blues' and is viewed as a combative role in which the police protect 'good guys' from the 'bad guys'.*
- *Cynicism – The police deal with some very inhuman aspects of life. This leads them to develop a cynical interpretation of their immediate surroundings and the criminals that they police.*
- *Pessimism – Linked to the cynicism is a pessimism, which typically places the police as a beleaguered minority.*

Suspicion

Operational policing is characterised by the need to be alert for signs of trouble, danger and evidence/intelligence. Thus the police develop finely grained cognitive maps of the social world so that they can readily predict and deal with the behaviour of others in different contexts without losing authority. This can result in suspicion and mistrust of certain social groups, resulting in stereotyping.
The critical issue is not the existence of stereotyping but the extent to which it is reality-based rather than being applied in a discriminatory and counter-productive manner.

Conservatism

Evidence has demonstrated that police officers are conservative, not necessarily just in the political meaning, but that they are more authoritarian and intolerant of liberal behaviour. They prefer crime control strategies where they can enforce the law and there is little negotiation for non-conformity.

Machismo

The police world is permeated by machismo which has become embedded in the recruitment and promotion processes. Policing was traditionally viewed as a 'job for the boys'. It has been argued that both the excessive alcoholic and sexual indulgences of the police are a product of machismo.

Isolation and solidarity	*The social isolation of the police has arisen from shift-work, erratic hours, aspects of the discipline code, tension from the job, covert knowledge they have about the community and a general hostility from some members of the community. Solidarity is the product of isolation as well as the nature of policing. Police rely on each other in dangerous situations. In addition, conflicts and division within the organisation lead to solidarity between departments and ranks.* *This creates an 'us and them' outlook where 'them' can either be other police departments or ranks, or community groups that need to be targeted and policed. These groups are exemplified by their worst characteristics and behaviours in order to define their relationships with them. Seven key groups have been identified:*

- *Good class villains – are professional, or experienced, criminals who are worth pursing.*
- *Police property – are typically those low-status and power-less groups that have at times been portrayed as distasteful or problematic. The prime function of the police is to control and segregate these groups to keep the streets safe. Legislation can effectively create new police property.*
- *Rubbish – are people who make calls that are seen as messy, intractable, unworthy of attention or the complainant's own fault. Domestic violence was once regarded as rubbish.*
- *Challengers – are people who routinely penetrate the secrecy of the police culture and challenge their decision-making and control. These may include other agencies, the legal profession and the media.*
- *Disarmers – are groups that may receive special sympathy police treatment because of their vulnerability. They may include women, children and the elderly.*
- *Do-gooders – are anti-police activists who challenge police authority and autonomy.*
- *Politicians – while they have the power to make the law, they are also viewed as not understanding the world of policing.*

Racial prejudice	*Arising from police conservatism comes racial prejudice, for example police suspicions and hostility towards minority groups. This can be illustrated vividly in numerous riots between the police and ethnic minority groups. The Scarman and MacPherson reports both highlighted racial prejudice within policing.*
Pragmatism	*Police operations are about providing an immediate response to a crisis or perceived crisis. Therefore a necessary pragmatism develops to deal with such circumstances. However a by-product of pragmatism is a lack of innovation and experimentation within the craft of policing.*

There are two competing theories for police culture. One is that people with the above characteristics choose a career in policing. The other is that these behaviours and attitudes are learnt and socialised in the nature of police work (Chan 1997; Waddington 1999). Research has demonstrated that, on recruitment, the attitudes of student officers differ little from those present in broader society. However, the probationary two years provide a period of socialisation in which initial attitudes almost invariably change as a result of exposure to 'cop culture' (Fielding 1998).

Police culture is not monolithic and manifests itself in differing forms both within and between forces. Informal rules and behaviours are not clear-cut or articulated but are embedded in specific practices and understandings according to situational and organisational circumstances.

Characterising police culture often overlooks that police work in reality is usually routine, mundane and administratively based. Nonetheless, police culture is a reflection of the power structures that exist in policing society. An understanding of how police view the social world and their role in it is crucial to the function of the police.

" How might cop culture influence the use of discretion by patrolling police officers? "

Answers should demonstrate a definition of organisational culture and its application to policing; how police use discretion; and examples of how organisational attitudes towards race, gender or human rights have been reflected in real life.

Taking it **FURTHER**

The issues of race and gender collide with cop culture, providing scope for further work either within the context of the police organisation or within the context of police/public interaction.

Textbook guide

CHAN J (1997) *Changing Police Culture: Policing in a Multi-cultural Society*, Cambridge: Cambridge University Press

NEWBURN T (2003) *Handbook of Policing*, Cullompton: Willan, especially Chapters 11, 21–23.

REINER R (2000) *The Politics of the Police* (3rd edn), Oxford: Oxford University Press

SILVESTRI M (2003) *Women in Charge: Policing Gender and Leadership*, Cullompton: Willan

WADDINGTON P (1999) 'Police (canteen) sub-culture: an appreciation', *British Journal of Criminology* 39 (2), pp. 286–309

YOUNG M (1991) *An Inside Job: Policing and Police Culture in Britain*, Oxford: Oxford University Press

2.19

race and diversity

Core areas: **Stephen Lawrence's racist murder**

Fundings of the 1999 public inquiry report (the eighth investigation or decision-making point)

Police Service of Northern Ireland diversity strategy

Greater Manchester diversity strategy

There has been widespread movement of different groups for thousands of years. Black soldiers were in the Roman army policing parts of Britain 2,000 years ago. Black and Jewish communities have existed on these islands for a 1,000 years at least. There has been tension between different religious groups for hundreds of years, not least in Ireland. There have been other tensions generated by the victimisation of people because of their gender, sexual orientation, age or ethnicity as well as race or religion.

Running themes

The perspectives of both **police organisations** and police officers and staff have come under detailed scrutiny in relation to race and diversity. The experiences and perspectives of ethnic and other minorities as **police officers and staff**, **victims, suspects, witnesses, third parties** and **the wider community** in general are particularly significant and should be borne in mind when answering essays and assignments. How do police organisations compare with **other agencies**? What can **statistical data** tell us about the policing of race and the management of diversity by the police both within the community and within their own organisation? What is the **political significance** of race and diversity?

Key thinkers

Lord Scarman laid the groundwork for the next three decades of policing diversity and race with his report on the Brixton disorders (Scarman, Lord L.G. (1981) *The Brixton Disorders 10–12 April 1981*, Cmnd 8427, London: HMSO).

Sir William MacPherson and his advisers, Dr John Sentamu, now Archbishop of York, Tom Cook, a former Deputy Chief Constable, and Dr Richard Stone, a Jewish philanthropist and GP, took wide-ranging evidence about the state of race relations and policing at the turn of the century (MacPherson W (1999) *The Stephen Lawrence Inquiry*, Cm 4262, London: HMSO).

Sir William Morris OJ and his colleagues, including Annesta Weekes QC, who had been counsel to the Stephen Lawrence Inquiry, developed themes from there to a new independent inquiry applying current thinking to professional standards and employment matters involving black officers in the Metropolitan Police (Morris W et al. 2004 *The Case for Change: An Independent Inquiry into Professional Standards and Employment Matters in the Metropolitan Police*, London: Metropolitan Police Authority).

Lord Laming and his adviser Detective Superintendent John Fox applied some of the Stephen Lawrence thinking across other services in partnership with policing, not least in their development of an open mind, healthy scepticism and an investigative approach when race and diversity meet child protection and murder (Laming, Lord (2003) *The Victoria Climbié Inquiry,* Cm 5730, London: HMSO).

This section examines policing in a society of many races and much diversity using the perspectives offered from one important milestone – *The Stephen Lawrence Inquiry Report* (MacPherson 1999).

Several reasons dictate this. First, the 70 recommendations of the public inquiry either directly relate to or touch upon every important aspect of race and diversity. Secondly, the report is available on the web. Thirdly, the report, its impact and its consequences have far-reaching effects for policing beyond race and diversity. Fourthly, there was widespread and almost unanimous agreement with the findings, and revulsion at the failures from across political parties, government, tabloid and broadsheet media and television. Fifthly, concern about the case has continued unabated for 13 years. A BBC television programme broadcast on 26 July 2006 (*The Boys Who Killed Stephen Lawrence*) received headline coverage across the media, including four- and five-page spreads in some papers. Sixthly, this is by far the best known and most widely discussed cause célèbre about policing failures and difficulties for a decade and forms a valuable case study, project or dissertation topic as a tribute to Stephen and his parents. It is an important topic and is of great relevance to other aspects considered in this study guide (e.g. the function and role of police (section 2.2), governance, structure and accountability (section 2.3), philosophies of policing (section 2.5) and criminal investigation (section 2.10)).

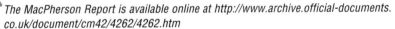

The MacPherson Report is available online at http://www.archive.official-documents. co.uk/document/cm42/4262/4262.htm
Related documents are available at http://police.homeoffice.gov.uk/community-policing/ race-diversity/stephen-lawrence-inquiry?version=1

Stephen Lawrence's racist murder

On 22 April 1993, just after 10.30 pm, Stephen and his friend Dwayne Brooks, having spent an evening together playing computer games, travelled home via a series of bus journeys which took them to Well Hall Road, Eltham, London SE9. There, a group of violent, racist young men, abused them, chased them, stabbed Stephen to death and terrorised Dwayne.

The initial police actions at the scene and nearby were found by the public inquiry to be grossly inadequate; the initial investigation was marred by missed opportunities and failed investigative potential. Over 20 different sources of information gave the police the names of the perpetrators within a few days but action was slow and eventually police charges were dropped by the CPS.

There are at least 11 investigations and reviews or decision-making points which failed to deliver justice to Mr and Mrs Lawrence and Dwayne Brookes. These were miscarriages of justice.

The eleven inquiries into Stephen Lawrence's racist murder

1　The original murder investigation for the first three days.
2　The continuing investigation by the second senior investigating officer. Charges discontinued by CPS.
3　The Mellish investigation that successfully prosecuted the father of one of the suspects.
4　The private prosecution bought by Mr and Mrs Lawrence. Charges were dismissed at the Old Bailey.
5　The inquest.
6　The Kent Police investigation carried out for the Police Complaints Authority.
7　The follow-up inquiry by the Metropolitan Police to the lines of inquiry suggested by the Kent police.
8　The public inquiry.
9　Operation Athena-Tower, a new inquiry into the murder. Insufficient evidence for the Crown Prosecution Service.
10　Civil actions by Mr and Mrs Lawrence and Dwayne Brooks.
11　A reactivated investigation following a BBC inquiry on 26 July 2006.

Findings of the 1999 public inquiry report (the eighth investigation or decision-making point)

The finding that attracted most attention and debate was that the police were institutionally racist (see boxes below). Other findings related to incompetence and dysfunctional practices.

Institutional racism

The Stephen Lawrence Inquiry (1999, para 6.34) defined institutional racism as 'a collective failure of the police service to deliver an appropriate and professional service due to their unwitting prejudice, ignorance, thoughtlessness or stereotyping that disadvantaged people because of their colour, culture or ethnic origin. It was seen or detected in the processes, attitudes and behaviour of the police during the investigation into Stephen's murder and in the evidence given to the inquiry.'

> ***Common pitfall:*** *Many students, and indeed police officers, politicians and journalists do not understand the difference between institutional and institutionalised racism.*
> *Institutional racism is a collective failure due to unwitting prejudice, ignorance, thoughtlessness or stereotyping that disadvantage people because of their colour, culture or ethnic origin.*
> *On the other hand, institutionalised racism is the overt or covert racism, through processes and practices of an organisation, however defended or explained, that disadvantage people because of their colour, culture or ethnic origin. In other words, the organisation knows that it is acting in this manner. There is nothing unwitting about it.*

However 18 of the 70 recommendations (25%) made by MacPherson directly relate to families and their relationships with communities, or to families and communities and their relationships with the police. This generated a massive increase in the numbers of trained police family liaison officers (700 were trained in the Metropolitan Police in the four years after the report was published) and developments in management and skills within this specialism. There had been untrained family liaison officers on every murder squad for many years. Research work by Avon and Somerset Constabulary had prepared the way for the required specialism. The inquiry report added dimensions regarding the sensitivity required by family liaison officers to deal with minority groups. This can be seen to benefit a wider range of the general and diverse population than a shortsighted reading of the inquiry report might have suggested.

Community involvement in family liaison training is derived from a wider recommendation about involving communities in many other aspects of policing. Looking back from the milestone of the report, there had been numerous attempts at improving relations with minority groups by increasing understanding and sensitivity. The work undertaken after Stephen's inquiry findings was by far the widest-ranging and most practical. For example, one criticism of the investigation had been the lack of overall interaction between different parts of policing, uniform, CID, specialisms, leadership. This gave rise to a new way of thinking about police activity – *critical incident management*. A nationwide training programme was developed using immersive learning and debriefing processes. A system of Gold Groups to oversee strategic aspects of potential or actual critical incidents has been established.

Community voices, critical friends of policing, called *independent advisers,* were introduced into both the training and the operational

Gold Groups to help think through the experiences and perceptions of policing of different communities and generate solutions and avoid problems. One aspect of this thinking developed into a new specialism, *community impact assessment*, a risk analysis and management task fulfilled by either police community specialists and/or intelligence officers.

Another aspect of the consequences of the inquiry recommendations that benefited all aspects of diversity was the development of *community safety units*. These units deal with a range of minority or special victims groups, possibly the best known of which is the investigation of hate crimes. Other recommendations dealt with the contentious issue of stop and search and recruitment and retention concerns.

As a further indicator of the importance that government, Parliament, the media and others placed on the issues disclosed a month after publication of the report, the then Home Secretary, Jack Straw, published an action plan that was notable for its strategic introduction and detailed tactical, performance-driven programme of activities.

HMIC has undertaken several thematic inspections in relation to diversity, including:

Winning the Race

http://inspectorates.homeoffice.gov.uk/hmic/inspect_reports1/thematic-inspections/winning-the-race/

Winning the Race – Revisited

http://police.homeoffice.gov.uk/news-and-publications/publication/community-policing/winning_race_revisited1.pdf

Embracing Diversity

http://inspectorates.homeoffice.gov.uk/hmic/inspect_reports1/thematic-inspections/wtr3-int.pdf

---

These reports and five years of work on the Home Secretary's action plans gave a framework for diversity strategies in individual forces. We will consider two now: the Police Service of Northern Ireland and Greater Manchester Police. The former, though coming from a different set of precursor problems, applied some of the Stephen Lawrence thinking (Patten C (1999) *A New Beginning: Policing in Northern Ireland*, Belfast: HMSO).

Police Service of Northern Ireland diversity strategy

The Police Service of Northern Ireland (PSNI) identify the background issues of two different community traditions in Northern Ireland (Protestant and Catholic), but they also consider in their strategy race, gender, disability, older people, mental health, travellers' concerns, gay/bisexual/transgender/transsexual issues, refugee and asylum seekers, youth, and other different faith and religious issues. The PSNI builds activities on a fundamental social, moral, legal and leadership framework to champion the rights and responsibilities that go with policing such a complex diverse mix. This they describe as not so much a 'wind of change' but as gale force activity to combat prejudice and hate, dealing with people according to their needs, applying human rights thinking and valuing the diversity of their own staff and communities.

Greater Manchester diversity strategy

The Race Equality Scheme (Amended) for the Greater Manchester Police (GMP) (2002/05) describes a negative impact assessment tool for diversity. This process and concepts are as relevant to individual black and ethnic minor officers (BEM) officers inside the service as to outside groups.

Part 4 of the scheme reads as follows:

ASSESS ANY LIKELY IMPACT.

This stage lies at the heart of the impact assessment process. Your starting point will be any disparities or potential disparities you have identified during the above process. You now have to make a judgement as to whether these amount to adverse impact. This involves systematically evaluating the proposed policy against all the information and evidence you have assembled and are using as a benchmark, and making a reasonable judgement as to whether the policy is likely to have significant negative consequences for a particular diverse group or groups. (GMP Race Equality Scheme (Amended), GMP 2002/05)

This is a helpful way to look generally at assessment and adverse impact in any policing, diversity or grievance procedure anywhere.

❝ What lessons might the Stephen Lawrence Inquiry have for community policing during the 'war on terror'? ❞

This explores the student's ability to identify the wider application of key lessons at a time of heightened racial tension (e.g. the utilisation of community impact assessments).

Taking it **FURTHER**

The Stephen Lawrence Inquiry Report and inquiry transcript contain a mass of material in respect of race and diversity. Was it racism, and if so what kind of racism, or incompetence that failed Mr and Mrs Lawrence? Is the emphasis on Stephen's murder and the subsequent inquiry justified?

The report of Sir William Morris OJ and his colleagues proposes a route map for valuing diversity and race when considering matters of grievance or otherwise *within* the police. He suggests changes within the following seven categories of behaviour:

1. Enhancing the office of constable and employment issues.
2. People issues, including the use of the ACAS Code and mediation.
3. Managing difference.
4. Governance, accountability and scrutiny.
5. Professional standards, including case management of internal investigations.
6. Capacity to deliver.
7. Building capacity.

MacPherson W (1999) *The Stephen Lawrence Inquiry,* Cm 4262, London: HMSO

Morris W (2004) *The Case for Change: An Independent Inquiry into Professional Standards and Employment Matters in the Metropolitan Police,* London: Metropolitan Police Authority

Textbook guide

BENYON J (ED.) (1984) *Scarman and After*, Oxford: Pergamon
BOWLING B & PHILLIPS C (2003) 'Policing ethnic minority communities', in T Newburn (ed.), *Handbook of Policing*, Cullompton: Willan, pp. 528–55
HOLDAWAY S (1996) *The Racialisation of British Policing*, Basingstoke: Macmillan
SPALEK B (ED.) (2002) *Islam, Crime and Criminal Justice*, Cullompton: Willan

2.20
gender and policing

Core areas: **History of women police**
Policing women victims

Running themes

The perspectives of both **police organisations** and police officers and staff have come under detailed scrutiny in relation to gender. The experiences and perspectives of women from ethnic majorities and minorities as **police officers and staff**, **victims**, **suspects**, **witnesses**, **third parties** and **the wider community** in general are particularly significant and should be borne in mind when answering essays and assignments. How do police organisations compare with **other agencies** in their treatment of female staff and of female victims? What can **statistical data** tell us about the policing and management of gender by the police both within the community and within their own organisation? What is the **political significance** of gender in policing?

History of women police

The Metropolitan Police Act 1829 decreed that all officers should be 'fit males' and this remained for almost the following 75 years. The turn of the twentieth century saw the emergence of feminist thinkers (Margaret Damer Dawson, Mary Allen and Nina Boyle) advocating the employment of female officers. The first female to be sworn in and given powers of arrest was Edith Smith in 1915 in Grantham. The First World War saw the development of the Women Police Volunteers, whose role was philanthropic: preserving the moral well-being of both women and soldiers at a time of social dislocation. There was then established a paid and sworn Women Police Service (WPS), whose role was to police female workers at munitions factories. They wore uniforms and campaigned to gain the status of 'sworn officers'. These early roles were primarily pastoral as there was still universal consensus that women did not have the physique or stamina to undertake full-time traditional crime patrol work.

The WPS remained separate until after the Second World War. The service had its own rank structure but was accountable to all-male upper ranks. Pay was lower, their uniforms were different and they were never armed. The numbers of female officers doubled during the Second World War from 282 to 418, and had reached almost 4,000 (almost 4% of the total force strength) before integration with the regular constabularies in 1975. Integration came about following the Labour government's insistence that the police should not be exempt from the Sexual Discrimination Act (1975). Thus reform was driven from external pressure rather than from within the service.

In 1981 women police officers accounted for 8.6% of the total police force of England and Wales. By 1993 this had risen to 13.2%. These figures were not equally distributed across the 43 forces and there were marked regional differences, from 9.2% in South Wales to 16.1% in the West Midlands. The first female assistant chief constable was appointed in 1983, with three more in 1994, while 1995 symbolised the end of the traditional male dominance with the first appointment of a female chief constable (Lancashire Police).

These figures have been partly explained by the recruitment process in that fewer women apply to become police officers, which in turn may relate to the perceived cult of masculinity and the nature of leadership in policing. Many female officers have been forced either to embrace this male culture as their own or fulfil the more traditional expectations associated with their role. These have been referred to as strategies of being *POLICEwomen* or *policeWOMEN*.

A step towards the consolidation of women in policing came with the formation of the British Association of Women Police (BAWP) in 1987. Its main objective is to enhance the role and understanding of the specific needs of the women who are employed as police officers. They have also been responsible for the development of the *gender agenda*, which is concerned with issues affecting women officers and their ability to achieve their potential within the service. It also recognises that other females in civilian support roles, and men, experience similar challenges.

While the gender agenda recognises and credits the police organisation for the progress achieved in the last decade, it also notes the 'failure to recognise the impact and consequences of the predominating and dominating culture on minority groups'. It also refers for the need to acknowledge the 'macho culture'. Numerous documented data attest to the persistence of various forms of traditional cop culture, often manifested in harassment, together with a range of coping strategies and resources for female officers.

The gender agenda

The gender agenda has five key aims:

1. For the police service to demonstrate consistently that it values women officers.
2. To achieve a gender, ethnicity and sexual orientation balance across the rank structure and specialisms consistent with the proportion of women in the economically active population.
3. To have a woman's voice in influential policy fora focusing on both internal and external service delivery.
4. To develop an understanding of the competing demands in achieving a work/life balance and a successful police career.
5. To have a working environment and equipment of the right quality and standards to enable women officers to do their job professionally.

It has been argued that the sexual discrimination case of Alison Halford, which was supported by the Equal Opportunities Commission and accompanied by intense media coverage, acted as a catalyst for change in 1992. Alison Halford was the first woman to reach the rank of assistant chief constable (in 1983) and became widely known as the most senior police woman in Britain. Yet after nine attempts, she failed to achieve further promotion. With the backing of the Equal Opportunities Commission, she took the police authorities to law. Her story documented the humiliation and disparagement she had to endure in an attempt to force her to relent and end her case. At the industrial tribunal, she was cross-examined for a fortnight in a case that was abandoned before her opponents were subjected to the same treatment. Alison Halford was awarded a significant settlement but the justice of her case remained unchallenged, as did her integrity. Alison Halford's case revealed the extent of male domination in the police force and the inadequacy of both internal and external procedures to address gender-based grievances.

The use of unlawful covert surveillance conducted against Halford by her senior male colleagues resulted in a landmark ruling at the European Court of Human Rights about the need for legislation to allow telephone tapping in the UK.

Halford v UK [1997] 24 European Human Rights Report 523

Policing women victims

The original 'caring and social' role of the pioneering female officers was the policing and chaperoning of female and juvenile suspects and offenders. This focused generally on policing the disreputable activities of females and promoting moral reform. In the late twentieth century their role shifted to the 'social policing' of violence involving women and children rather than vice, including domestic violence, sexual assault, rape and the physical and sexual abuse of children – crimes that were not previously viewed as serious enough for a conventional police response.

It has been argued that the police response to female and child victims, particularly those listed above, during the 1980s was as much a response to secure public support for policing as to address victims' needs. A much publicised 1982 BBC documentary about the handling of a rape complainant by Thames Valley Police proved a catalyst for significant procedural changes, including the establishment of rape victim suites throughout England and Wales. Despite a continuing increase in rape allegations reported to the police over the last two decades, the rate of conviction remains unchanged. Of the 11,766 allegations of rape made in 2002 there were only 655 convictions (5.6%), 258 having come from guilty pleas. Only 14% of investigated cases result in trial. Similarly, the police have also responded to incidents of domestic violence and child abuse where the emphasis has been to take these crimes more seriously and develop specialist departments, skills and procedures.

"Compare and contrast the issues faced by female officers in the organisational culture of the police with those faced by officers from ethnic minorities."

This question draws upon two aspects of diversity: gender and race. It requires an exposition of the organisational culture before considering the issues of gender and race. An answer might focus on selection procedures for specialist posts or promotion as a case study.

Taking it **FURTHER**

Building on the sample question above, what role has leadership to play in defining culture and gender issues in the police service?

Textbook guide

BAIRD REPORT (1921) *Minutes of Evidence: Committee on the Employment of Women on Police Duties*, Cmd 1133, London: HMSO
HALFORD A (1993) *No Way Up the Greasy Pole*, London: Constable
HEIDERSOHN F (1992) *Women in Control? The Role of Women in Law Enforcement*, Oxford: Oxford University Press
SILVESTRI M (2003) *Women in Charge: Policing, Gender and Leadership*, Cullompton: Willan
WESTMARLAND L (2001) *Gender and Policing*, Cullompton: Willan

2.21	
the police and the media	

Core areas: **Police use of media**
Public perceptions from drama (Dixon's legacy)
Media influences on policing
Police self-portraiture in the media

Running themes

Consider how the following have been portrayed in the various media. To what end and to whose advantage or disadvantage? What **political agendas** are at play? How are **statistics** presented, used (or abused)? Whose perspective is being presented – and what alternative (and contradictory?) perspectives are relevant: the **police organisation, police officers and staff, victims, suspects, witnesses** and **third parties**, and **other agencies**? When the views of **the wider community** are presented, just how representative are those views? Does the media have an agenda?

Police use of media

The relationship between the police and media has always been complex and interdependent. Factual and fictional representation of the police, by the media, influences and shapes public perception, not only about policing but also about law and order more generally. The first police press office was established in 1919 at Scotland Yard. An official police spokesperson these days is more likely to be a civilian than a serving police officer. The professionalisation of the police spokesperson role culminated in the establishment of the Association of Police Public Relations Officers in 1998.

It has been argued that the police–media relationship disproportionately concentrates on the serious, the sensational and the solved. This is exemplified by the programme *Crimewatch* or by police appealing to the community for information, calm or support. *Crimewatch* was first broadcasted in 1984 and is based upon case reconstruction. Although it attracts over 6 million viewers, it has sparked considerable debate regarding its use of dramatic reconstruction and, consequently, its contribution to the fear of crime. Most of the cases portrayed focus on crimes against the person. The programme requires police participation and access to police files.

Case study

The interrelationship between the media and the police can be traced and understood in the cases of the disappearance of Holly Wells and Jessica Chapman. As the inquiry transformed from a missing persons inquiry to an

(Continued)

(Continued)

abduction and murder investigation, the relationship between the police and the media illustrated the immediacy and intensity of the situation with fluid, fast-time reporting. Cambridgeshire police were praised for the way in which they handled the media, and in keeping the inquiry in the public domain. However, they were soon to experience what has been termed the 3 Es of police–media relations:

- Expectation
- Exhortation
- Excoriation

Whenever the police would do something, or appear to do something wrong, the media would publicly excoriate them, having the power to present the police as either villains or heroes. The Soham case illustrated the fine line that exists between a police-led story and a media-driven investigation. (Leishman & Mason 2003)

'Primary definers', the experts with privileged access to the media, such as senior police officers, academics and MPs, use the media to construct the news and shape and influence the policing agenda. This can lead to the development of a 'moral panic' where traditional street offences are converted into a new virulent form of crime, such as the mugging epidemic of the early 1970s which the media principally associated with young black males as perpetrators.

Public perceptions from drama (Dixon's legacy)

The iconic fictional character typifying the 'golden age' of British policing is Dixon of Dock Green, who encapsulated a quintessential community style of policing crime and criminals. Dixon was portrayed as a proud, tea-drinking cheery bobby patrolling the street in his uniform, keeping the public safe from harm. The powerful message conveyed by the programme was that of honesty, community spirit and crime does not pay; criminals were caught and the harm done to victims redressed. These principles were reinforced through an explicit moral conclusion that was presented at the end of each programme. This image of policing was replaced in the 1970s by harder-hitting series like *Z Cars* and *The Sweeney*, where the British bobby no longer embodied all that was considered good and proper. Human fallibility was portrayed by a faster detective style of policing, with elements of noble cause corruption, rule-breaking, prejudice and that not all crime could be solved.

Juliet Bravo and the *Gentle Touch* were the first series to depict females in senior police roles and challenged the police culture that had been portrayed in other series. Up to this point women had been portrayed as victims, molls, vamps, wives or mothers. A key feature of *Juliet Bravo* was its emphasis on procedural accuracy. This quasi-documentary approach to detail was expanded in *The Bill*. *The Bill* defines the virtual territory of policing, where the moral certainties of Dixon are gone and police officers' virtues are relative rather than absolute. The topics presented in the programme reflect the current concerns and issues of policing in society. While police dramas have portrayed different styles and perceptions of policing over the decades, with narratives becoming more complex, the police officer on the beat has generally remained the heroic face of routine law enforcement.

> **Common pitfall:** When discussing TV portrayals of policing, students should make efforts to view tapes of old programmes otherwise any discussion will inevitably suffer from a lack of direct observation and first-hand research. To rely solely on secondary literature for such assignments means students will be discussing other people's interpretations, not the portrayals themselves.

Media influences on policing

Reiner et al. (2000) revealed a three-fold increase in newspaper coverage of central crime stories from between 7% and 9% during the period 1945–51 to around 21% between 1985 and 1991. The tabloid papers, such as *The Sun*, exhibited the highest increase. In addition, certain types of crime were over-represented, such as sex crimes and personal violence, which do not necessarily reflect the official statistics.

As well as influencing public endorsement of the police and policing, the media representations can challenge and contest the actions of the police. The conviction of Peter Sutcliffe, the murder of Stephen Lawrence and the shooting of Jean Charles de Menezes all generated media challenges to police action and accountability. Roger Graef's series of *Police* documentaries in 1982 was a seminal and ground-breaking fly-on-the-wall examination of the Thames Valley Police. His film, *An Allegation of Rape*, changed the way the police dealt with rape victims.

More recently, in the BBC's *Secret Policeman* (2003), the undercover reporter Mark Daly exposed the racist behaviour of police recruits. The *Secret Policeman* sent shockwaves through every police force in the country when it was broadcast in October 2003. It was presented in the media as proof of remaining racism throughout the police service despite the lessons from the Stephen Lawrence inquiry. In fact, it was evidence of racism in the society from which the recruits were drawn. The recruitment process has not eliminated those with racist attitudes. Those exhibiting racist behaviour were immediately dismissed. Whether or not police diversity training would have changed their behaviour (which arguably it should have done) will remain an unanswered question. The documentary, filmed only in one police training centre, provided evidence of one issue but was interpreted as providing evidence of a related but discrete issue across the entire service. It was this second interpretation to which the police service nationally responded.

The documentary was to have a profound influence on police policy and practice in relation to recruitment and training nationally. In January 2004, the Greater Manchester Police (the force infiltrated by Daly) launched its Respect Programme, which is aimed in part at tackling racism and the diversity issues raised by *The Secret Policeman*.

The media have a crucial role in defining public perceptions and, consequently, through their response to public perceptions, police behaviour. Both fictional and factual media presentations can illuminate that which would otherwise be inaccessible to the public, thus providing an informal accountability mechanism. Media interest in policing is also maintained and exacerbated by the political agenda, where law and order has become a primary priority for government.

Police self-portraiture in the media

There remains one further aspect of the relationship between the police and the media: the self-portraits painted by serving or retired police officers exploiting media outlets. This is articulated in two different types of autobiography: the conventional autobiography published in book format, usually at the end of a career which, in most cases (and particularly those of retired chief constables or commissioners), the reader will be invited to regard as distinguished; and secondly, in the form of an internet blog. The latter, of course, is a relatively recent phenomenon and neither form has been the subject of concerted serious study as far as the present authors are aware.

Blogging raises some important issues. It can be, and usually is, undertaken anonymously. Thus contentious views can be expressed with little fear of reprisal or even verification and accountability. It can either be the expression of a single author's opinion or it can develop into a chat-room or bulletin-board format with numerous views expressed and issues debated. The lack of effective regulation means that it is difficult to prevent the creation and dissemination of erroneous assertions and misconceptions and it may be difficult to distinguish between fatuous contributions and the useful posting of good practice ideas.

One thing is certain, while the official autobiographies attempt to define and determine 'history' as viewed from the perspective of the author, blogging creates a spontaneous and fluid historical archive. The quality of neither format is assured and as sources for studying the police, both should be viewed with circumspection. What message is the author, or authors, trying to convey, and why?

❝ In 2000 the *News of the World* launched a name-and-shame campaign to ensure that convicted and released paedophiles were identified to the communities in which they were resident. Evaluate the outcome of this campaign in terms of the consequences for community policing. ❞

There are a number of different approaches that could be adopted. The primary issue is the management of persons who have previously committed dangerous offences and have completed their sentence in the community: what are the risks of such people re-offending and how can the risk be managed? Alternatively, answers could focus on the violent vigilantism that the campaign ignited, which resulted in innocent men being forced from their homes, suicides, violent assaults, murders and widespread public disorder.

Taking it **FURTHER**

Combining this subject with research methodology, consider which has been more effective at changing police behaviour: the overt Thames Valley Police documentary or the covert infiltration by undercover reporter Mark Daly. What ethical issues arise?

Textbook guide

KIDD-HEWITT D & OSBORNE R (EDS) (1996) *Crime and the Media: The Post-Modern Spectacle*, London: Pluto

LEISHMAN F & MASON P (2003) *Policing and the Media: Facts, Fictions and Factions*, Cullompton, Willan

MAWBY R (2002) *Policing Image: Policing, Communication and Legitimacy in Modern Britain,* Cullompton: Willan

REINER R (2003) 'Policing and the Media' in T. Newburn (ed.), *Handbook of Policing,* Cullompton: Willan

part three*
study and revision skills

*in collaboration with David McIlroy

3.1

general introduction

This chapter better equips you to profit from lectures, benefit from seminars, construct essays efficiently, develop effective revision strategies and respond comprehensively to exam pressures. The six sections comprise checklists and bullet points focusing attention on key issues, exercises promoting active learning, illustrations and analogies anchoring learning principles in everyday events and experiences, worked examples demonstrating features such as structure, headings and continuity, and tips providing practical advice in nutshell form.

Readers can decide how much effort to invest in each exercise, according to individual preferences and requirements. Some of the points in the exercises will be covered in the text either before or after the exercise. You may prefer to read each section right through before going back to tackle the exercises. Suggested answers are provided in italics after some of the exercises, so avoid these if you prefer to work through the exercises on your own. The aim is to prompt reflection on the material, aid recall of what has been read, and trigger your own thoughts. Space is provided to write responses down in a few words. Writing will help you to slow down and digest the material and may also enable you to process the information at a deeper level of learning.

The overall aim of the chapter is to facilitate academic and personal development. These twin emphases are stressed throughout. By giving attention to these factors, you will give yourself the toolkit you will need to excel in your studies.

3.2

how to get the most out of your lectures

This section will help you:

- Make the most of your lecture notes
- Prepare your mind for new terms
- Develop an independent approach to learning
- Write efficient summary notes from lectures
- Take the initiative in building on your lectures

Keeping in context

According to higher education commentators and advisers, best-quality learning is facilitated when it is set within an overall learning context. It should be the responsibility of your tutors to provide a learning context, but it is your responsibility to understand this overall context, even before your first lecture begins. Such a panoramic view can be achieved by becoming familiar with the outline content of both a given subject and the entire study programme. Before each lecture briefly remind yourself of where it fits into the overall scheme of things. Think, for example, of how you feel more confident when you move into a new city (e.g. to attend university) once you become familiar with your bearings, that is where you live in relation to college, shops, stores, buses, trains, places of entertainment, etc.

The same principle applies to your course – find your way around the study programme, locating the position of each lecture within the overall framework.

Use of lecture notes

It is always beneficial to do some preliminary reading before a lecture. If lecture notes are provided in advance (e.g. electronically), then print these out, read over them and bring them with you to the lecture. You can insert question marks on issues where you will need further clarification. Some lecturers prefer to provide full notes, some prefer to make skeleton outlines available and some prefer to issue no notes at all! If notes are provided, take full advantage and supplement these with personal notes as you listen. Humans possess ability for 're-learning savings', (i.e. it is easier to learn material the second time around), as it is evident that we have a capacity to hold residual memory deposits. So some *basic preparation will afford great advantage* – you will be able to 'tune in' and think more clearly about the lecture than you would have done without the preliminary work.

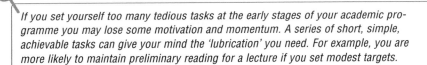

If you set yourself too many tedious tasks at the early stages of your academic programme you may lose some motivation and momentum. A series of short, simple, achievable tasks can give your mind the 'lubrication' you need. For example, you are more likely to maintain preliminary reading for a lecture if you set modest targets.

Mastering technical terms

Assume that in an early lecture you are introduced to a series of new terms such as 'paradigm', 'empirical' and 'zeitgeist'. New words can be threatening, especially if you have to face a string of them in one lecture. The uncertainty about the new terms may impair your ability to benefit fully from the lecture and therefore hinder learning quality. Some subjects require technical terms and the use of them is unavoidable.

In terms of learning new words, it will be very useful to work out what they mean from their context when you first encounter them. This often works better than might first be imagined. It would also be very useful to obtain a small indexed notebook and use this to build up a glossary of terms. In this way you could include a definition of a word, an example of its use, where it fits into a theory and any practical application of it.

Checklist for mastering terms used in your lectures

✓ Read lecture notes before the lectures and list any unfamiliar terms
✓ Read over the listed terms until you are familiar with their sound

✓ Try to work out meanings of terms from their context
✓ Do not suspend learning the meaning of a term indefinitely
✓ Write out a sentence that includes the new word (do this for each word)
✓ Meet with other students and test each other with the technical terms
✓ Jot down new words you hear in lectures and check out the meaning soon afterwards

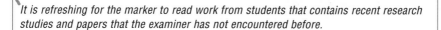

Confidence will greatly increase when you begin to follow the flow of arguments that contain technical terms and when you can freely and accurately use these terms when speaking and writing.

Developing independent study

Current educational ethos focuses on the twin aims of cultivating team-work/group activities and independent learning. There is not necessarily a conflict between the two, as they should complement each other. Students committed to independent learning have more to offer other students when working in small groups. Guidelines given in lectures are designed to facilitate deeper independent study, providing direction and structure for extended personal pursuit. *Your aim should invariably be to build on what you are given: never think of merely returning the bare bones of the lecture material in a course work essay or exam.*

It is refreshing for the marker to read work from students that contains recent research studies and papers that the examiner has not encountered before.

Note-taking strategy

Note-taking in lectures is an art that can be perfected with practice. Each student should find the formula that works best for him or her. What works for one may not work for another. Some students can write more quickly than others, some are better at shorthand than others and some are better at deciphering their own scrawl! The problem will always be to try to find a balance between concentrating beneficially on what you hear and making sufficient notes that will enable you to comprehend later what you have heard. Do not become frustrated by the fact that you will not understand or remember immediately everything you have heard.

> *Being present at a lecture and paying attention to what you hear will give you a considerable advantage over those students who do not attend.*

Checklist for note-taking in lectures

✓ Develop the note-taking strategy that works best for you
✓ Work at finding a balance between listening and writing
✓ Make some use of optimal shorthand (e.g. a few key words may summarise a story)
✓ Too much writing may impair the flow of the lecture for you
✓ Too much writing may impair the quality of your notes
✓ Some limited notes are better than none
✓ Good note-taking may facilitate deeper processing of information
✓ It is essential to 'tidy up' notes as soon as possible after a lecture
✓ Reading over notes soon after lectures will consolidate your learning

Developing the lecture

The value of lectures is undermined if they are merely a mode of 'passive learning' and students approach lectures in the wrong way. Lecturers can devise ways of making lectures more interactive, for example, with interactive handouts, by posing questions during the lecture and giving time out for students to reflect on these, by short discussions at given junctures in the lecture, or by using small groups within the session. Ensure that you are not merely a passive recipient of information by taking steps to develop the lecture yourself. A list of suggestions is presented below to help you take the initiative in developing the lecture content.

Checklist to ensure that the lecture is not merely a passive experience

✓ Try to interact with the lecture material by asking questions
✓ Highlight points that you would like to develop in personal study
✓ Trace connections between the lecture and other parts of your study programme
✓ Bring together notes from the lecture and other sources
✓ Restructure the lecture outline into your own preferred format
✓ Think of ways in which aspects of the lecture material can be applied
✓ Design ways in which aspects of the lecture material can be illustrated
✓ If the lecturer invites questions, make a note of all the questions asked
✓ Follow up on issues of interest that have arisen out of the lecture

> *You can contribute to this active involvement in a lecture by engaging with the material before, during and after it is delivered.*

EXERCISE

You might now like to summarise (and/or add) some factors that would help you to capitalise fully on the benefits of a lecture

✓ ....
✓ ....
✓ ....
✓ ....
✓ ....

3.3

how to get the most out of your seminars

This section will help you to:

- Be aware of the value of seminars
- Focus on links to learning
- Recognise qualities you can use repeatedly
- Manage potential problems in seminars
- Prepare yourself adequately for seminars

Not to be underestimated

Seminars are sometimes optional in a degree programme and are therefore poorly attended because they are underestimated. Some students may be convinced that the lecture is the truly authoritative way to receive quality information. Undoubtedly, lectures play an important role in an academic programme, but *seminars have a unique contribution to learning that will complement lectures*. Other students may feel that their time would be better spent in personal study. Again, private study is unquestionably essential for personal learning and development, but you will nevertheless diminish your learning experience if you neglect seminars. If seminars were to be removed from academic programmes, then something really important would be lost.

Checklist – some useful features of seminars

- ✓ They can identify problems that you had not thought of
- ✓ They can clear up confusing issues
- ✓ They allow you to ask questions and make comments
- ✓ They can help you develop friendships and teamwork
- ✓ They enable you to refresh and consolidate your knowledge
- ✓ They can help you sharpen motivation and redirect study efforts

An asset to complement other learning activities

In higher education there is currently emphasis on variety – variety in delivery, learning experience, learning styles and assessment methods. The seminar is deemed to hold an important place within the overall scheme of teaching, learning and assessment. In some programmes, the seminars are directly linked to the assessment task. Whether or not they have such a place in your course, they will provide you with a unique opportunity to learn and develop.

Seminars offer a variety of contributions, different perspectives and emphases. They offer the chance to interrupt and the experience of being interrupted! It is a safe environment in which to explore ideas (and make mistakes!). When one student admits that they did not understand an important piece of information, other students frequently acknowledge the same. Learning to ask questions and not feel stupid ensures that seminars will be an asset for learning and a life-long educational quality.

Creating the right climate in seminars

We have one mouth to talk, but two ears to listen. One potential problem with seminars is that some students may take a while to learn this lesson, and other students may have to help hasten them on the way (graciously but firmly!). In lectures, your main role is to listen and take notes, but in seminars a balance must be struck between listening and speaking. It is important to make a beginning in speaking even if it is just to repeat something that you agree with. You can also learn to disagree in an agreeable way. For example, you can raise a question against what someone else has said and pose this in a good tone. For example, 'If that is the case, does that not mean that ...'. In addition, it is perfectly possible to disagree with others by avoiding personal attacks. For example, 'that was a really stupid thing to say', or 'I thought you knew better than that', or 'I'm surprised that you don't know that by now' are not the most diplomatic ways of disagreeing. It is important to have the right climate in which to learn; avoiding unnecessary conflict will foster such a climate.

Suggest what can be done to reach agreement (set ground rules) that would keep seminars running smoothly and harmoniously

✓ ....
✓ ....
✓ ....
✓ ....
✓ ....

Some suggestions – Appoint someone to guide and control the discussion. Invite individuals to prepare a contribution in advance. Hand out agreed discussion questions at some point prior to the seminar. Stress at the beginning that no one should monopolise the discussion and emphasise that there must be no personal attacks on any individual (state clearly what this means). Invite and encourage quieter students to participate and assure each person that his or her contribution is valued.

Links in learning and transferable skills

To progress from shallow to deep learning it is important to develop the capacity to make connections between themes or topics and across subjects. This also applies to the various learning activities, such as lectures, seminars, fieldwork, computer searches and private study. Another factor to think about is: 'What skills can I develop, or improve on, from seminars that I can use across my study programme?' For instance, key skills include the ability to communicate and the capacity to work within a team. These are transferable skills that can be utilised throughout your course, but you are not likely to develop them in a lecture.

Write out or think about (a) three things that give seminars value, and (b) three useful skills that you can develop in seminars

(a)

✓ ....
✓ ....
✓ ....

(b)

✓ ....

✓ ....

✓ ....

A key question that you should bring to every seminar is 'How does this seminar connect with my other learning activities and my assessments?'

An opportunity to contribute

Those who have never made a contribution to a seminar before may need an 'ice breaker'. It does not matter if a first contribution is only a sentence or two – the important thing is to make a start. One way to do this is to make brief notes as others contribute, and while doing this, a question or two might arise in your mind. If your first contribution is a question, that is a good start. Or it may be that you will be able to point out some connection between what others have said, or identify conflicting opinions that need to be resolved. If you have already begun making contributions, it is important to keep the momentum going. Do not lapse back into the safe cocoon of shyness.

EXERCISE

See if you can suggest how you might resolve some of the following problems that might hinder you from making a contribution to seminars:

- One student who dominates and monopolises the discussion
- Someone else has already said what you really want to say
- Fear that someone else will correct you and make you feel stupid
- Feel that your contribution might be seen as short and shallow
- A previous negative experience puts you off making any more contributions

---

Strategies for benefiting from your seminar experience

Delivering seminar presentations is discussed more fully in a complementary study guide (McIlroy 2003). Here it will suffice to present some useful summary checklists.

Checklist – how to benefit from seminars

✓ Do some preparatory reading
✓ Familiarise yourself with the main ideas to be addressed
✓ Make notes during the seminar
✓ Make a verbal contribution, even if it is only asking a question
✓ Remind yourself of the skills you can develop
✓ Trace learning links from the seminar to other subjects/topics on your programme
✓ Make brief bullet points on what you should follow up on
✓ Read over your notes as soon as possible after the seminar
✓ Continue discussion with fellow students after the seminar has ended

Checklist – how to benefit if you are required to give a presentation

✓ Have a practice run with friends
✓ If using visuals, do not obstruct them
✓ Check out beforehand that all equipment works
✓ Space out points clearly on visuals (large and legible)
✓ Time talk by visuals (e.g. 5 slides by 15 minute talk = 3 minutes per slide)
✓ Make sure your talk synchronises with the slide on view at any given point
✓ Project your voice so that all in the room can hear
✓ Inflect your voice and do not stand motionless
✓ Spread eye contact around audience
✓ Avoid twin extremes of fixed gaze at individuals and never looking at anyone
✓ It is better to fall a little short of your time allocation than to run over it
✓ Be selective in what you choose to present
✓ Map out where you are going and summarise the main points at the end

3.4

essay writing tips

This section will help you to:

- Quickly engage with the main arguments
- Channel your passions constructively
- Note your main arguments in an outline
- Find and focus on your central topic questions
- Weave quotations into your essay

Getting into the flow

Essay writing requires your mind to be active and engaged with your subject. You can 'warm up' for your essay by tossing the ideas to and fro within your head before you begin to write. This will allow you to think within the framework of your topic, and this will be especially important if you are coming to the subject for the first time.

The tributary principle

As a tributary stream flows into a main river meandering to the sea, so every idea introduced in an essay should move towards the overall theme addressed. Ideas might be relevant to a sub-heading that is in turn relevant to a main heading. In addition to tributaries, there can also be 'distributaries', which are streams that flow away from the river. In an essay these would represent the ideas that run away from the main stream of thought and leave the reader trying to work out what their relevance may have been. It is one thing to have grasped your subject thoroughly, but quite another to convince your reader that this is the case. The aim should be to build up ideas sentence by sentence and paragraph by paragraph until the clear purpose has been communicated to the reader.

> *Good essay writing requires not only the inclusion of relevant material but linking statements showing the connections to the reader.*

Listing and linking the key concepts

Subjects usually have central concepts that can sometimes be labelled by a single word. Course textbooks may include a glossary of terms and these provide a direct route to the efficient mastery of a topic. The central words or terms are the essential raw materials that can be built upon. Ensure that you learn the words and their definitions, and that you can go on to link the key words together so that in your learning activities you will add understanding to your basic memory work.

> *List key words under general headings when possible and logical. You may not always see the connections immediately but when you return to a problem that previously seemed intractable, the connections may well present themselves.*

Example – Write an essay on 'Aspects and perceptions of different roles in policing'

You might decide to draft your outline points in the following manner (or you may prefer to use a mind map approach):

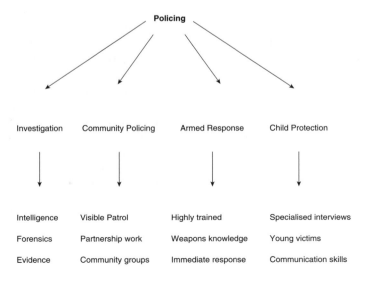

Investigation	Community Policing	Armed Response	Child Protection
Intelligence	Visible Patrol	Highly trained	Specialised interviews
Forensics	Partnership work	Weapons knowledge	Young victims
Evidence	Community groups	Immediate response	Communication skills

An adversarial system

Higher education students are required to make the transition from descriptive to critical writing. The critical approach looks at both sides of an argument, like a law case which has a prosecution and a defence. Objectivity, transparency and fairness are primary concerns. No matter how passionately you may feel about a given cause, you must not allow information to be filtered out because of personal prejudice. An essay must not be a one-sided crusade. Awareness of alternative views must be demonstrated in an even-handed manner and these views should be represented as accurately as possible.

> *The writer's role is like that of the judge ensuring that all the evidence is heard, and that nothing will compromise either party.*

Stirring up passions

The above points do not of course mean that you are not entitled to a personal persuasion or to feel passionately about your subject. Such feelings may well be a marked advantage if they can be controlled and channelled into balanced, effective writing (see example below). Some students may be struggling at the other end of the spectrum, being required to write about a topic that they feel quite indifferent about. As you engage with your topic and toss the ideas around in your mind, you will hopefully find that your interest is stimulated, if only at an intellectual level initially.

> *It is important for a large project or dissertation that you choose a topic for which you can maintain motivation, momentum and enthusiasm.*

Here is an example of an issue that may stir up passions: *arguments for and against the existence of God.*

For

- Universe appears to have a design
- Humans have an innate desire to worship

- Humans are free to choose good or evil
- Common threads between religions
- Religion provides strong moral foundations
- Individuals report subjective experiences
- God's revelation is in holy books

Against

- There are flaws in the universe
- Not all appear to have the desire to worship
- How can evil be adequately explained?
- Many religions and diverse beliefs
- Humanists accept moral principles
- Subjective experiences are not infallible
- Devout people differ in interpretation

Structuring an outline

Inspiration to write on a given subject must be channelled into a structure that will allow the inspiration (and the quality of the work) to be communicated clearly to the reader (and the marker). It is a basic principle in all walks of life that *structure and order facilitate good communication*. For example, an essay plan might include an introduction, a conclusion, three main headings and several sub-headings (see example below). Headings might not be included in the final presentation, having just been used initially to structure and balance the arguments. Once the outline is drafted, this can be easily sketched into an introduction, and you will have been well prepared for the eventual conclusion.

A good structure helps balance the weight of each argument against another, and arranges your points in the order that will best facilitate the fluent progression of your argument.

Example – write an essay that compares and contrasts policing in England and Wales and that in Scotland

1. Police Powers

(a) PACE does not apply in Scotland
(b) Scottish police witnesses must be corroborated
(c) Anglo-Scottish cross-border powers

2. Inter-force relations

(a) Eight forces in Scotland, 43 in England and Wales
(b) SOCA operates in the UK, SDEA operates in Scotland
(c) There is a greater degree of central service collaboration in Scotland
(d) ACPO/ACPO(S) relations with government

3. Relationships with other criminal justice professionals

(a) Different court systems and procedures
(b) Different functions for Crown Prosecutors and Procurators Fiscal
(c) Different historical and legal traditions

Finding major questions

Without losing sight of the essay question that has been set – and which must therefore be answered in order to achieve marks – when constructing a draft outline for an essay or project, identify and list the major issue or issues that you might wish to tackle. The ability to design a good enabling question upon which to base an answer to the essay question is an art form that should be cultivated, and such questions will allow you to impress your assessor with the quality of your thinking.

> *Constructing ideas around key questions helps focus the mind to engage effectively with the subject. You will be like a detective, exploring the evidence and investigating the findings.*

To illustrate the point, consider the example presented below. If you were asked to write an essay about the effectiveness of the police in your local community you might, as your starting point, pose the following questions.

Example – The effectiveness of the police in the local community: initial questions

- Is there a high-profile police presence?
- Are there regular 'on the beat' officers and patrol car activities?
- Do recent statistics show increases or decreases in crime in the area?
- Are the police involved in community activities and local schools?
- Does the local community welcome and support the police?
- Do the police have a good reputation for responding to calls?
- Do the police harass people unnecessarily?

- Do minority groups perceive the police as fair?
- Do the police have an effective complaints procedure to deal with grievances against them?
- Do the police solicit and respond to local community concerns?

Rest your case

The aim should be to give the clear impression that your arguments are not based entirely on hunches, bias, feelings or intuition. *In exam answers and essays, assertions made and arguments used must be supported by evidence, the provenance of which is properly cited.* By the time the assessor reaches the end of your work, he or she should be convinced that your conclusions are evidence-based. A fatal flaw to be avoided is to make claims for which you have provided no authoritative source.

> *Give the clear impression that what you have asserted is derived from recognised, up-to-date sources. Spread citations across an essay and not just in one or two paragraphs at the beginning or end.*

Some examples of how you might introduce your evidence and sources are provided below:

According to Flood (2004) .....
Ashworth (2002) has concluded that .....
Johnson (1992) found that ...
It has been claimed by Maguire (2003) that .....
Fielding (1995) asserted that .....
A review of the evidence by Tilley (2003) suggests that .....
Findings from a meta-analysis presented by Wall (2001) would indicate that .....

It is sensible to vary the expression used to avoid monotony and repetition, and it also aids variety to introduce researchers' names at various places in the sentence (not always at the beginning). It is advisable to choose the expression that is most appropriate – for example you can make a stronger statement about reviews that have identified recurrent and predominant trends in findings as opposed to one study that appears to run contrary to all the rest.

> *Credit is given for the use of caution and discretion when this is clearly needed.*

Careful use of quotations

Although it is desirable to present a good range of cited sources, it is not judicious to present these as a 'patchwork quilt' in which what others have said is cut and pasted together with little interpretative comment or coherent structure. In general, avoid very lengthy quotes – short ones can be very effective. Aim at blending the quotations as naturally as possible into the flow of your sentences. It is also good to vary your practices, sometimes using short, direct, brief quotes, and at other times summarising the gist of a quote in your own words. The source for an argument you have summarised or a quote you have used must be cited with the author's name, year of publication and page reference. *Failure to cite properly will arouse suspicions of plagiarism.*

> *Use quotes and evidence in a manner that demonstrates you have thought the issues through and have integrated them in a way that demonstrates you have been focused and selective in your use of sources.*

In terms of referencing, practice may vary from one discipline to the next, but some general points that will go a long way in contributing to good practice are:

- If a reference is cited in the text, it must also be included in the bibliography or list of references at the end of the essay (and vice versa).
- Names and dates in the text should correspond exactly with those listed in the references or bibliography.
- The references or bibliography should be listed in alphabetical order by the surname (not the initials) of the author or first author.
- Any reference cited in the text must be traceable by the reader.

Plagiarism, or the unattributed copying of someone else's work and passing it off as one's own work, is an academic 'crime'. It is easily done in this age of electronic resources and 'cut-and-paste' word-processing functions,

(Continued)

although simple copying from a book is also plagiarism. It contravenes the regulations of every higher education institution. Punishments vary but can include expulsion, the denial of a degree or the loss of all marks for the piece of work in which plagiarism is discovered. Lecturers have access to numerous software tools that can detect plagiarism. Above all, plagiarism is evidence of:

- dishonesty; and/or
- intellectual inability to meet required higher education academic standards

A clearly defined introduction

An essay's introduction should define the problem or issue being addressed and set it within context. Resist the temptation to elaborate on any issue at the introductory stage. The introduction should merely signpost the main themes discussed in the body of the essay.

Leaving the introduction until the end of your writing will ensure the introduction accurately maps out what has been written.

EXERCISE

For practice, look back at the drafted outline on examining the policing differences between England and Wales and Scotland. Try to design an introduction for that essay in about three or four sentences

Conclusion – adding the finishing touches

In the conclusion, the essay themes should be tied together in a clear and coherent manner. It is the last opportunity to identify where the strongest evidence points or where the balance of probability lies and so leave a positive overall impression in the reader's mind. The conclusion to an exam question often has to be written hurriedly under the pressure of time, but with an essay (course work) there is time to reflect on, refine and adjust the content to your satisfaction. The goal should be a smooth finish that does justice to the range of content in summary and succinct form. Do not underestimate the value of an effective conclusion. 'Sign off' your essay in a manner that brings closure to the treatment of your subject.

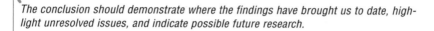

The conclusion should demonstrate where the findings have brought us to date, highlight unresolved issues, and indicate possible future research.

Top-down and bottom-up clarity

An essay gives you the opportunity to refine each sentence and paragraph on your word processor. Each sentence is like a tributary that leads into the stream of the paragraph that in turn leads into the main stream of the essay. From a 'top-down' perspective (i.e. starting at the top with your major outline points), clarity is facilitated by the structure you draft in your outline. Ensure that the sub-headings are appropriately placed under the most relevant main heading, and that both sub- and main headings are arranged in a logical sequence. From a 'bottom-up' perspective (i.e. building up the details that 'flesh out' your main points), check that each sentence is a 'feeder' for the predominant concept in a given paragraph. When all this is done, check that the transition from one point to the next is smooth rather than abrupt.

Checklist – summary for essay writing

- ✓ Before you start, have a 'warm up' by tossing the issues around in your head
- ✓ List the major concepts and link them in a fluent form
- ✓ Design a structure (outline) that will facilitate balance, progression, fluency and clarity and make sure it answers the question that has been set
- ✓ Pose supplementary questions and address these in a critical fashion
- ✓ Demonstrate that your arguments rest on evidence and spread cited sources across your essay
- ✓ Provide an introduction that sets the scene and a conclusion that rounds off the arguments
- ✓ DO NOT PLAGIARISE

Attempt to write (or at least think about) some additional features that would help facilitate good essay writing

✓ ....

✓ ....

✓ ....

✓ ....

✓ ....

In the above checklist, you could have features such as originality, clarity in sentence and paragraph structure, applied aspects, addressing a subject you feel passionately about and the ability to avoid going off on a tangent.

3.5

revision hints and tips

This section will help you to:

- Map out your accumulated material for revision
- Choose summary tags to guide your revision
- Keep well-organised folders for revision
- Make use of effective memory techniques
- Use a revision technique that combines bullet points and in-depth reading
- Profit from the benefits of revising with others
- Attend to the practical exam details that will help keep panic at bay
- Use strategies that keep you task-focused during the exam
- Select and apply relevant points from your prepared outlines

The return journey

A return journey will usually pass by all the same places already passed on the outward journey. Landmarks observed on the outward journey will be recalled by the returning traveller. Similarly, revision is a means to 'revisit' what you have encountered before. Familiarity with the material can help reduce anxiety, inspire confidence and fuel motivation for further learning and good performance.

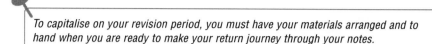

To capitalise on your revision period, you must have your materials arranged and to hand when you are ready to make your return journey through your notes.

Start at the beginning

Revision strategies should be on your mind from your first lecture at the beginning of the academic semester. Do not waste any lecture, tutorial, seminar, group discussion, etc. by letting the material evaporate into thin air. Get into the habit of making a few guidelines for revision after each learning activity. Keep a folder, or file, or little notebook that is reserved for revision and write out the major points learned. By establishing this regular practice you will find that what you have learned becomes consolidated in your mind, and you will also be in a better position to 'import' and 'export' your material both within and across subjects.

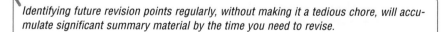

Identifying future revision points regularly, without making it a tedious chore, will accumulate significant summary material by the time you need to revise.

Compile summary notes

It is useful and convenient to have a little notebook or cards on which outline summaries can be written that provide an overview of the subject at a glance. You could also use treasury tags to hold different batches of cards together while still allowing for inserts and resorting. Such practical resources can easily be slipped into your pocket or bag and be produced when you are on the bus or train, or while sitting in a traffic jam. A glance over your notes will consolidate your learning and will also activate your mind to think further about your subject. Make note of the questions that you would like to think about in greater depth. Your primary task is to get into the habit of constructing outline notes that will be useful for revision, and a worked example is provided below.

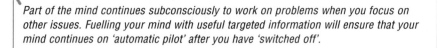

> *Part of the mind continues subconsciously to work on problems when you focus on other issues. Fuelling your mind with useful targeted information will ensure that your mind continues on 'automatic pilot' after you have 'switched off'.*

Example – part of a course on communication is the use of non-verbal communication, and your outline revision structure for this might be as follows

1 Aspects of non-verbal communication that run parallel with language

    (a)   Pauses
    (b)   Tone of voice
    (c)   Inflection of voice
    (d)   Speed of voice

2 Facets of non-verbal communication related to use of body parts

    (a)   How close to stand to others
    (b)   How much to use the hands
    (c)   Whether to make physical contact (e.g. touching, hugging, hand shake)
    (d)   Extent and frequency of eye contact

3 General features that augment communication

    (a)   Use of smiles and frowns
    (b)   Use of eyebrows
    (c)   Expressions of boredom or interest
    (d)   Dress and appearance

Keep organised records

The twin skills of time and task management are key to a successful career. Academic training is a useful preparation for this. Failure to cultivate these skills inhibits personal potential. Keep a folder for each subject and divide the subject topic by topic in the same order in which they are presented in course lectures. Bind them together in a ring binder or folder and use subject dividers to keep them apart. Make a numbered list of the contents at the beginning of the folder, and list each topic clearly as it marks a new section in your folder. Place all your notes on a given topic within the appropriate section. Don't put off this simple task, do it straight away. Notes may come from lectures, seminars, tutorials, library reading, internet searches, personal notes, etc. It is also essential that when you remove these for consultation that you return them to their 'home' immediately after use.

Academic success has as much to do with good organisation and planning as it has to do with ability. The value of the quality material you have accumulated on your academic programmes may be diminished because you have not organised it into an easily retrievable form.

Use past papers

Revision will be very limited if it is confined to memory work. As well as reading over your revision cards/notebook it is also essential that you become familiar with previous exam papers so that you will have some idea of how the questions are likely to be framed. Build up a good range of past exam papers (especially recent ones) and add these to your folder.

Reviewing previous exam questions will help fact/argument recollection and an understanding of the issues. Past exam questions, and questions you develop for yourself, will aid revision.

Example – evaluate the advantages and disadvantages of creating regional police forces

Immediately, you can see that you will require two lists and you can begin to work on documenting your reasons under each, as below:

Advantages

- Enhanced provision of 'protective services'
- Economies of scale
- Increased uniformity of systems and equipment
- Better strategic understanding of regional criminality
- Enhanced political status in relation to the Home Office

Disadvantages

- Diversion of resources from urban to rural areas (or vice versa)
- Reduction in neighbourhood policing provision
- Loss of local political control
- Loss of local identity between force and community
- Loss of ACPO jobs

Notice the word 'evaluate' is in the question – you must make judgements. You may decide to work through advantages first and then the disadvantages, or it may be your preference to compare point by point as you go along. Conclusions may be down to (evidenced) personal subjective preference but at least all the issues will have been worked through from both standpoints. Revision should include critical thinking as well as memory work.

> *You cannot think adequately without the raw materials invested in your memory.*

Employ effective mnemonics (memory aids)

'Mnemonics' can be simply defined as aids to memory. They are devices that will help you to recall information that might otherwise be difficult to retrieve from memory. For example, an old toy in the attic may suddenly trigger a flood of childhood memories associated with it. Mnemonics can be thought of as keys that open the memory's storehouse.

Visualisation is one technique that can be used to aid memory. For example, the location method is where a familiar journey is visualised and you can 'place' the facts that you wish to remember at various landmarks along the journey (e.g. a bus stop, a car park, a shop, a store, a bend, a police station, a traffic light, etc.). This has the advantage of making an association of the information to be learnt with other material that is already firmly embedded and structured in your memory. Therefore, once the relevant memory is activated, a dynamic 'domino effect' will be triggered. There is a whole toolkit of mnemonics. Some examples and illustrations of these are presented below.

> Arranging subject matter in a logical sequence will ensure your series of facts will connect with each other and trigger other relevant recollections. Memory devices can be used at either the stage of initial learning or for later revision.

Location method – defined above.

Visualisation – this technique turns information into pictures. For example, a question about the problems and pleasures of pets could be envisaged as two tug-of-war teams that pull against each other. Each player could be visualised as an argument with the label written on his or her tee-shirt. The contest could start with two players and then be joined by another two and so on. Each player's weight could be compared to the strength of each argument. You might also want to make use of colour to distinguish contrasting perspectives.

Alliteration's artful aid – find a series of words that all begin with the same letter (e.g. Recall, Recognition, Reconstruction and Re-learning) as a strategy for boosting memory.

Peg system – 'hang' information on to a term so that when you hear the term you will remember the ideas connected with it (an umbrella term). In the example on ageing there were four different types – biological, chronological, sociological and psychological. Under biological you could remember menopause, hair loss, wrinkling, vision loss, hearing deterioration, etc.

Hierarchical system – this is a development of the previous point with higher-order, middle-order and lower-order terms. For example, you could think of the continents of the world (higher order), and then group these into the countries under them (middle order). Under countries you could have cities, rivers and mountains (lower order).

Acronyms – take the first letter of all the key words and make a word from these. An example from business is SWOT – Strengths, Weaknesses, Opportunities and Threats.

Mind maps – these have become very popular. They allow you to draw lines that stretch out from the central idea and to develop the subsidiary ideas in the same way. The method has the advantage of giving you the complete picture at a glance, although they can become a complex work of art!

Rhymes and chimes – words that rhyme and words that end with a similar sound (e.g. commemoration, celebration, anticipation). These provide another dimension to memory work by including sound. Memory can be enhanced when information is processed in various modalities (e.g. hearing, seeing, speaking, visualising).

Alternate between methods

It is not sufficient to present outline points in response to an exam question (although it is better to do this than nothing if you have run out of time in your exam). Substance, evidence and arguments must be added to the basic points. You should work at finding the balance between the two methods – outline revision cards might be best reserved for short bus journeys, whereas extended reading might be better employed for longer revision at home or in the library. The ultimate goal should be to bring together an effective, working approach that will enable you to face your exam questions comprehensively and confidently.

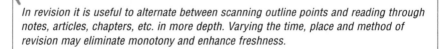

In revision it is useful to alternate between scanning outline points and reading through notes, articles, chapters, etc. in more depth. Varying the time, place and method of revision may eliminate monotony and enhance freshness.

Example – imagine that you are doing a course on police investigation

Your major outline topics might be:

- Crime scene examination
- Intelligence framework
- Witness identification and interviewing
- Stop and search
- Custody procedures
- Investigation management

This outline would be your overall, bird's eye view of the course. You could then choose one of the topics and have all your key terms under that. For example, under custody procedures you might have listed: arrest, arrival at custody suite, identification, interviewing, charge, bail.

In order to move from memory to understanding you would need to consider the journey through the custody suite.

Alternating between memory work and reading will soon enable you to think through the processes just by reviewing your outlines.

Revising with others

A revision group may provide another fresh approach to the last stages of your learning. First, ensure that others carry their workload and are not merely using the hard work of others as a short-cut to success. Group sessions should be used in conjunction with personal study. This collective approach enables you to assess your strengths and weaknesses (showing you where you are off-track), and to benefit from the resources and insights of others. Group participants can design questions for the whole group to address. The group can also go through past exam papers and discuss the points that might provide an effective response to each question. It should not be the aim of the group to provide standard and identical answers for each group member to mimic.

Individuals should aim to use their own style and content while drawing on and benefiting from the group's resources.

EXERCISE

Make a list of the advantages and disadvantages of revising in small groups

Advantages   Disadvantages

1. ....

2. ....

3. ....

4. ....

5. ....

Can the disadvantages be eliminated or at least minimised?

Checklist – good study habits for revision time

- ✓ Set a date for the 'official' beginning of revision and prepare for 'revision mode'
- ✓ Do not force cramming by leaving revision too late
- ✓ Take breaks from revision to avoid saturation
- ✓ Indulge in relaxing activities to give your mind a break from pressure
- ✓ Minimise or eliminate the use of alcohol during the revision season
- ✓ Get into a good rhythm of sleep to allow renewal of your mind
- ✓ Avoid excessive caffeine, especially at night, so that sleep is not disrupted
- ✓ Try to adhere to regular eating patterns
- ✓ Try to have a brisk walk in fresh air each day (e.g. in the park)
- ✓ Avoid excessive dependence on junk food and snacks

EXERCISE

Write your own checklist on what you add to the revision process to ensure that it was not just a memory exercise

- ✓ ....
- ✓ ....
- ✓ ....
- ✓ ....
- ✓ ....

In the above exercise, additions to memory work during revision might include using past exam papers, setting problem-solving tasks, doing drawings to show connections and directions between various concepts, explaining concepts to student friends in joint revision sessions, or devising your own mock exam questions.

3.6	
exam tips	

This section will help you to:

- Develop strategies for controlling nervous energy
- Tackle worked examples of time and task management in exams
- Attend to the practical details associated with the exam
- Stay focused on the exam questions
- Link revision outlines to strategy for addressing exam questions

Handling your nerves

Exam nerves are usual. Test anxiety arises because your performance is being evaluated, the consequences are likely to be serious and you are working under the pressure of a time restriction. However, focusing on the task at hand rather than on feeding a downward negative spiral in your thinking patterns will help you keep your nerves under control. In the run-up to your exams, practise some simple relaxation techniques that will help bring stress under control.

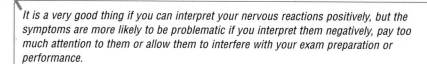

It is a very good thing if you can interpret your nervous reactions positively, but the symptoms are more likely to be problematic if you interpret them negatively, pay too much attention to them or allow them to interfere with your exam preparation or performance.

Practices that may help reduce or buffer the effects of exam stress

- Listening to music
- Simple breathing exercises
- Some muscle relaxation
- Watching a movie
- Enjoying some laughter

- Doing some exercise, e.g. a brisk walk
- Relaxing in a bath (with music if preferred)

The best choice is going to be the one (or combination) that works best for you – perhaps to be discovered by trial and error. Some of the above techniques can be practised on the morning of the exam, and even the memory of them can be used just before the exam. For example, you could run over a relaxing tune in your head, and have this echo inside you as you enter the exam room. The idea behind all this is, first, that stress levels must come down, and secondly, that relaxing thoughts will serve to displace stressful reactions. It has been said that stress is the body's call to take action, but anxiety is a maladaptive response to that call.

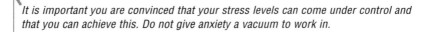

It is important you are convinced that your stress levels can come under control and that you can achieve this. Do not give anxiety a vacuum to work in.

Time management with examples

As you approach an exam it is all-important to develop the belief that you can control the situation. Work through the list of issues that must be addressed: tick them off one by one. It is important to understand before the exam the length of time you should allocate to each question. Sometimes this can be quite simple (although it is always necessary to read the rubric carefully). For example, if two questions are to be answered in a two-hour paper, you should allow one hour for each question. If it is a two-hour paper with one essay question and five shorter answers, you could allow one hour for the essay and 12 minutes each for the shorter questions. Always check the weighting of marks on each question, and deduct whatever time it takes you to read over the paper and to choose your questions. Practise using past papers. What time management strategy might apply in each of the following scenarios?

Check that the structure of your exam paper is the same as in previous years. Excessive time spent on your 'strongest' question may not compensate for very poor answers to other questions. Read the rubric carefully in the exam.

EXERCISE

Here are some examples for working out the division of exam labour by time

1. A 3-hour paper with 4 compulsory questions (equally weighted in marks).

2. A 3-hour paper with 2 essays and 10 short questions (each of the 3 sections carry one-third of the marks).

3. A 2-hour paper with 2 essay questions and 100 multiple-choice questions (half marks are on the 2 essays and half marks on the multiple choice section

---

Develop a calculating frame of mind and be sure to do the calculations before the exam. Ensure that the structure of the exam has not changed since the last one. Also deduct the time taken to read over the paper in allocating time to each question.

Suggested answers to previous exercise

1. *This allows 45 minutes for each question (4 questions × 45 minutes = 3 hours). However, allowing 40 minutes for each question will give you 20 minutes (4 questions × 5 minutes) to read over the paper and plan your outlines.*

2. *In this example you can spend 1 hour on each of the two major questions, and 1 hour on the 10 short questions. For the two major questions you could allow 10 minutes for reading and planning on each, and 50 minutes for writing. In the 10 short questions, you could allow 6 minutes in total for each (10 questions × 6 minutes = 60 minutes). However, if you allow approximately 1 minute reading and planning time, this leaves 5 minutes writing time for each question.*

3. *In this case you have to divide 120 minutes by 3 sections – allowing 40 minutes for each. You could allow 5 minutes reading/planning time for each essay and 35 minutes for writing (or 10 minutes reading/planning and 30 minutes writing). After you have completed the two major questions you are left with 40 minutes to tackle the 100 multiple-choice questions.*

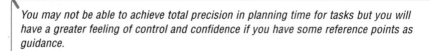

You may not be able to achieve total precision in planning time for tasks but you will have a greater feeling of control and confidence if you have some reference points as guidance.

Task management with examples

Having decided on the questions, the answers must be planned. Some students prefer to plan all outlines and draft work at the beginning, while others prefer to plan and address one answer before proceeding to address the next question. *Decide on your strategy before entering the exam room and stick to your plan.* On completing the draft outline as rough work, allocate an appropriate time for each section. This will prevent excessive treatment of some aspects while falling short on other parts. Careful planning will help you achieve balance, fluency and symmetry.

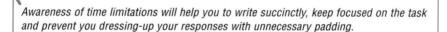

Awareness of time limitations will help you to write succinctly, keep focused on the task and prevent you dressing-up your responses with unnecessary padding.

Some students put as much effort into their rough work as they do into their exam essay.

An over-elaborate mind map may give the impression that that essay is little more than a repetition of this detailed structure, and that the quality of the content has suffered because too much time was spent on the plan.

EXERCISE

Work out the time allocation for the following outline, allowing for one hour on the question. Deduct 10 minutes taken at the beginning for choice and planning.

Discuss whether it is justifiable to ban cigarette smoking in pubs and restaurants.

1. **Arguments for a ban**

   (a) Health risks from sustained exposure to passive smoking
   (b) Employees (such as students) suffer unfairly
   (c) Children with parents may also be victims

2. **Arguments against a ban**

   (a) Risks may be exaggerated
   (b) Dangerous chemicals and pollutants in the environment are ignored by governments
   (c) Non-smokers can choose whether to frequent smoking venues

3. **Qualifying suggestions**

   (a) Better use of ventilation and extractor fans
   (b) Designated non-smoking areas
   (c) Pubs and restaurants should be addressed separately in relation to a ban

---

Attend to practical details

This short section summarises the practical details that should be attended to in preparation for an exam. There are always students who turn up late, or go to the wrong venue or go to the wrong exam, or do not turn up at all! *Check and re-check that you have all the details of each exam correctly noted.* Arriving late induces panic reactions and reduces the time available to answer the questions and gain marks.

> Attend the correct venue in good time so that you can quieten your mind and bring any stress under control.

Make note of the following details and check that you have taken control of each one.

Checklist – practical exam details

✓ Check you know the correct venue
✓ Make sure you know how to locate the venue before the exam day
✓ Ensure that the exam time you have noted is accurate

✓ Allow sufficient time for your journey and consider the possibility of delays

✓ Bring an adequate supply of stationery

✓ Bring a watch for your time and task management

✓ You may need some liquid such as a small bottle of still water

✓ You may also need to bring some tissues

✓ Observe whatever exam regulations your university/college has set in place

✓ Fill in the required personal details before the exam begins

Control wandering thoughts

A 1960s study found that students who frequently lifted their heads and looked away from their scripts during exams tended to perform poorly. It implied that the students were taking too much time out when they should have been on task. *One way to fail your exam is to get up and walk out of the test room, but another way is to 'leave' the test room mentally by being preoccupied with distracting thoughts.* Distracting thoughts divert you from the task at hand and debilitate your test performance. Read over the two lists of distracting thoughts presented below.

Typical test-relevant thoughts (evaluative)

- I wish I had prepared better
- What will the examiner think
- Others are doing better than me
- What I am writing is nonsense
- I can't remember important details

Characteristic test-irrelevant thoughts (non-evaluative)

- Looking forward to this weekend
- Which video should I watch tonight?
- His remark really annoyed me yesterday
- I wonder how the game will go on Saturday
- I wonder if he/she really likes me?

Research has consistently shown that distracting, intrusive thoughts during an exam are more detrimental to performance than stressful symptoms such as sweaty palms, dry mouth, tension, trembling, etc. Moreover, it does not matter whether the distracting thoughts are negative evaluations related to the exam or are totally irrelevant to the exam.

Checklist – practical suggestions for controlling wandering thoughts

✓ Be aware that this problem is detrimental to performance
✓ Do not look around to find distractions
✓ If distracted, write down 'keep focused on task'
✓ If distracted again, look back at above and continue to do this
✓ Start to draft rough work as soon as you can
✓ If you struggle with initial focus, then re-read or elaborate on your rough work
✓ If you have commenced your essay, re-read your last paragraph (or two)
✓ Do not throw fuel on your distracting thoughts – starve them by re-engaging with the task at hand

Links to revision

The revision guidelines above equip you with outline plans when entering the exam room. You may have chosen to use headings and subheadings, mind maps, hierarchical approaches or just a series of simple mnemonics. Whatever method you choose to use, you should be furnished with a series of memory triggers to aid recall once you begin to write.

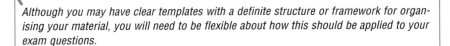

Although you may have clear templates with a definite structure or framework for organising your material, you will need to be flexible about how this should be applied to your exam questions.

For example, imagine that films are one of the topics that you will be examined on. You decide to memorise lists of films that you are familiar with under categorical headings in the following manner.

Romantic Comedy	*War/History/Fantasy*	*Space/Invasion*
Notting Hill	Braveheart	Star Wars
Pretty Woman	Gladiator	Independence Day
Along Came Polly	First Knight	Alien
Four Weddings and a Funeral	Troy	Men in Black

Adventure/Fantasy	*Horror/Supernatural*
Harry Potter	Poltergeist
Lord of the Rings	The Omen
Alice in Wonderland	Sixth Sense
Labyrinth	What Lies Beneath

The basic mental template might be these and a few other categories. You know that you will not need every last detail, although you may need to select a few from each category. For example, you might be asked to:

(a) compare and contrast features of comedy and horror
(b) comment on films that have realistic moral lessons in them
(c) comment on films that might be construed as a propaganda exercise
(d) identify films where the characters are more important than the plot and vice versa

Some questions will restrict the range of categories you can use (a), while others will allow you to dip into any category (b, c and d).

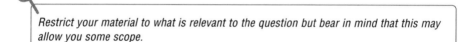

> Restrict your material to what is relevant to the question but bear in mind that this may allow you some scope.

Art of 'name dropping'

In most topics at university you will be required to cite studies as evidence for your arguments and to link these to the names of researchers, scholars or theorists. It will help if you can use the correct dates or at least the decades, and it is good to demonstrate that you have used contemporary sources, and have done some independent work. A marker will have dozens if not hundreds of scripts to work through and they will know if you are just repeating the same phrases from the same sources as everyone else. There is inevitably a certain amount of this that must go on, but there is room for you to add fresh and original touches that demonstrate independence and imagination.

> *Give the clear impression that you have done more than the bare minimum and that you have enthusiasm for the subject. Spread the muse of researchers' names throughout the essay rather than compressing them into the first and last paragraphs, for example.*

Flight, fight or freeze

The autonomic nervous system equips the body for flight or fight when faced with threatening situations – including an exam. Symptoms may include deep breathing, trembling, headaches, nausea, tension, dry mouth and palpitations. How should we react to these once they have been triggered? You are going into the exam room to 'tackle' the questions, and not to run away from the challenge before you.

The final illustration below uses the analogy of archery to demonstrate how you might take control in an exam.

Checklist – lessons from archery

✓ Enter the exam room with a quiver full of arrows – all the points you will need to use

✓ Eye up the target board you are to shoot at – choose the exam questions

✓ Stand in a good position for balance and vision – prepare your time management

✓ Prepare your bow and arrow and take aim at the target – keep focused on the task at hand and do not be sidetracked

✓ Pull the string of the bow back to get maximum thrust on the arrow – match your points to the appropriate question

✓ Aim to hit the board where the best marks are (bull's eye or close) – do not be content with the minimum standard such as a mere pass

✓ Pull out arrows and shoot one after another to gain maximum hits and advantage – do not be content with preparing one or two strong points

✓ Make sure your arrows are sharp and the supporting bow and string are firm – choose relevant points and support with evidence

✓ Avoid wasted effort by loose and careless shots – do not dress up your essay with unnecessary padding

Write your own checklist on the range of combined skills and personal qualities that you will need to be at your best in an exam

✓ ....
✓ ....
✓ ....
✓ ....
✓ ....

Skills might include such things as critical thinking, time and task management, focusing on the issues, and quickly identifying the problems to address. Personal qualities might include factors such as confidence, endurance, resilience and stress control.

3.7	
tips on interpreting essay and exam questions	

This section will help you to:

- Focus on the issues that are relevant and central
- Read questions carefully and take account of all the words
- Produce a balanced critique in your outline structures
- Screen for the key words that will shape your response
- Focus on different shades of meaning between 'critique', 'evaluate', 'discuss' and 'compare and contrast'

What do you see?

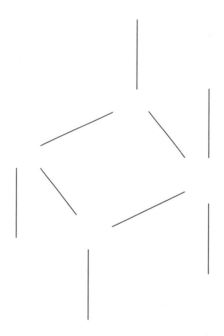

The human mind has a tendency to impose the nearest similar and familiar template on that which we think we see. (The two-dimensional arrangement of lines above, for instance, is often interpreted as a three-dimensional chair because our mind fills in the blanks.) The same can also apply to the way you read exam or essay questions.

Read, understand and answer the question that has been set. The phrasing of the question will give clues as to how the answer should be approached. Do not 'fill in the blanks' by answering a question that hasn't been asked.

This is especially likely if you have primed yourself to expect certain questions to appear in an exam, but it can also happen in coursework essays. Although examiners do not deliberately design trick questions, they cannot always prevent you from seeing things that were not designed to be there. When one student was asked what the four seasons are, the response given was 'salt, pepper, mustard and vinegar'. This was not quite what the examiner had in mind!

Go into the exam room, or address the coursework essay, well prepared. But be flexible enough to structure your learned material around the focus of the question.

Make sure that you answer the set question, although there may be other questions that arise out of this for further study that you might want to highlight in your conclusion. As a first principle you must answer the set question and not another question that you had hoped for in the exam or essay.

Do not leave the examiner feeling that, rather like politicians are said to do, you are evading the question.

Example – Discuss the strategies for improving community policing

Directly relevant points

- Visible patrol officers patrolling area
- Deploy Police Community Support Officers
- Increase local media campaigns
- Engage with local businesses and partners
- Identify what the community wants from the police
- Engage with local schools

Less relevant points

- Identify key crime problems and hotspots
- Campaign for additional police resources
- Identify areas for improvement in training
- Maximise resource allocation
- Identification of hidden community groups
- Maximise partnership working

Although some of the points listed in the second column may be relevant to strategies for improving community policing overall, they are not directly relevent to the community members. If the question had included the quality of policing then some of these issues should be given greater priority.

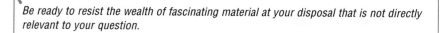

Be ready to resist the wealth of fascinating material at your disposal that is not directly relevant to your question.

Missing your question

A student bitterly complained after an exam that the topic he had revised so thoroughly had not been tested in the exam. The first response to that is that students should always cover enough topics to avoid selling themselves short in the exam – the habit of 'question spotting' is always a risky game to play. However, the reality in the anecdotal example was that the question the student was looking for was there, but he had not seen it. He had expected the question to be couched in certain words and he could not find these when he scanned over the questions in blind panic. Therefore, the simple lesson is *always read over the questions carefully, slowly and thoughtfully*. This practice is time well spent.

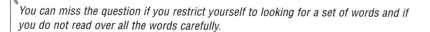

You can miss the question if you restrict yourself to looking for a set of words and if you do not read over all the words carefully.

Write it down

If you write down the question you have chosen to address, and perhaps quietly articulate it with your lips, you are more likely to process fully its true meaning and intent. Think how easy it is to misunderstand a question that has been put to you verbally because you have misinterpreted the tone or emphasis.

> *If you read over the question several times you should be aware of all the key words and will begin to sense the connections between the ideas and will envisage the possible directions you should take in your response.*

Take the following humorous example:

(a)   What is that on the road ahead?
(b)   What is that on the road, a head?

Question (a) calls for the identification of an object (what is that?), but question (b) has converted this into an object that suggests there has been a decapitation! Ensure, therefore, that you understand the direction the question is pointing you towards so that you do not go off at a tangent. One word in the question that is not properly attended to can throw you completely off track, as in the following example:

(a)   Discuss whether the love of money is the root of all evil.
(b)   Discuss whether money is the root of all evil.

These are two completely different questions as (a) suggests that the real problem with money is inherent in faulty human use – that is, money itself may not be a bad thing if it is used as a servant and not a master – whereas (b) may suggest that behind every evil act that has ever been committed money is likely to have been implicated somewhere in the motive.

Pursue a critical approach

In degree courses you are usually expected to write critically rather than merely descriptively, although it may be necessary to use some minimal descriptive substance as the raw material for your debate.

Example – Evaluate the evidence: Is police culture as a result of the organisation or the people attracted to policing itself?

Arguments for organisational culture

- Rank and file structure
- Immediate response to crisis

- Fewer female offices then male
- Crime fighting culture rather than enforcing the peace

Arguments for individuality

- Authoritarian people are more attracted to join the police
- Individuals are empowered with discretion
- Minimal supervision in many roles
- The sense of power conferred by the State on an individual officer
- Having a narrow view that policing is only about arresting criminals

Given that the question is about a critical evaluation of the evidence, the issues need to be addressed one by one from both standpoints. What you should not do is digress into a tangent about the physical characteristics of the Eagle lunar module or the astronauts' suits. Neither should you be drawn into a lengthy description of lunar features and contours, even if you have in-depth knowledge of these.

Analyse the parts

In an effective sports team the end product is always greater than the sum of the parts. Similarly, a good essay cannot be constructed without reference to the parts. Furthermore, the parts will arise as you break down the question into the components it suggests to you. Although the breaking down of a question into components is not sufficient for an excellent essay, it is a necessary starting point.

To achieve a good response to an exam or essay question, aim to integrate all the individual issues presented in a manner that gives shape and direction to your efforts.

Example 1 – discuss whether the preservation and continued investment in police–community consultation groups is justified

Two parts to this question are clearly suggested – preservation and continued investment. You need to do justice to each in your answer. Other issues that arise in relation to these are left for you to suggest and discuss. Examples might be alternative consultation methods, current statutory obligations, and performance accountability to central government.

Example 2 – evaluate the advantages and disadvantages of giving students course credit for participation in experiments

This is a straightforward question with two major sections – advantages and disadvantages. You are left with the choice of the issues to address, and can arrange these in the order you prefer. Ensure that you do not have a lop-sided view of this even if you feel quite strongly one way or the other.

Example 3 – trace in a critical manner western society's changing attitudes to the corporal punishment of children

Consider the role of governments, the church, schools, children's charities, parents and the media. Some reference points to the past are needed as you are asked to address the issue of change. There is scope to examine where the strongest influences for change arise and where the strongest resistance comes from. Are the changes dramatic or evolutionary?

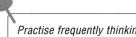

Practise frequently thinking of questions in this way – both with course topics and other subjects. Topics that are not on your course, but which really interest you, may be helpful in developing critical thinking skills.

Example – how much did the wealthy Scottish man leave behind?

A wealthy Scottish man died. No one in his village knew how much he had left behind. The issue was gossiped about for some time, but one man claimed that he knew how much the man had left. He teased the villagers night after night. Eventually he let his big secret out – the rich man had left 'all of it' behind! No one in the village had been able to work out the ruse because of the convergent thinking style they used. Some exam questions may require you to be divergent in the way you think (i.e. not just one obvious solution to the problem). This may require you to act like a detective in the way you investigate and solve problems. The only difference is that you may need to set up the problem as well as the solution!

> *Get into the habit of 'stepping sideways' and looking at questions from several angles. The best way to do this is to practise (e.g. utilising previous exam papers).*

Checklist – ensuring that questions are understood before being fully addressed

✓ Read over the chosen question several times
✓ Write it down to ensure that it is clear
✓ Check that you have not omitted any important aspect or point of emphasis
✓ Ensure that you do not wrongly impose preconceived expectations on the question
✓ Break the question into parts (dismantle and rebuild)

EXERCISE

Write your own checklist on any additional points of guidance for exams that you have picked up form tutors or textbooks

✓ ....
✓ ....
✓ ....
✓ ....
✓ ....

When asked to discuss

Students often ask how much of their own opinion they should include in an essay. In a discussion, when you raise one issue, another one can arise out of it. One tutor used to introduce his lectures by saying that he was going to 'unpack' the arguments. When you unpack an object (such as a new desk that has to be assembled), you first remove the overall packaging, such as a large box, and then proceed to remove the covers from all the component parts. All the parts must then be assembled, according to the given design, so that they hold together in the intended manner. In a discussion, your aim should be not just to identify and define all the parts that contribute, but also to show where they fit (or don't fit) into the overall picture.

Although the word 'discuss' implies some allowance for your opinion, remember that this should be evidenced opinion rather than groundless speculation, with direction, order and structure.

Checklist – features of a response to a 'discuss' question

✓ Contains a chain of issues that lead into each other in sequence
✓ Clear shape and direction is unfolded in the progression of the argument
✓ Underpinned by reference to findings and certainties
✓ Identification of issues where doubt remains
✓ Tone of argument may be tentative but should not be vague

If a critique is requested

One example that might help clarify what is involved in a critique is the hotly debated topic of the physical punishment of children. It would be important, in the interests of balance and fairness, to present all sides and shades of the argument. What evidence is there to support each argument? How might issues that have been coloured by prejudice, tradition, religion and legislation best be introduced? You would aim to identify emotional arguments, arguments based on intuition and to get down to those arguments that really have solid, evidence-based support. Finally you would want to flag up where the strongest evidence appears to lie, and you should also identify issues that appear to be inconclusive. You would be expected, if possible, to arrive at some certainties.

Write your own summary checklist for the features of a critique. You can either summarise the above points or use your own points, or a mixture of the two

✓ ....

✓ ....

✓ ....

✓ ....

✓ ....

If asked to compare and contrast

When asked to compare and contrast, you should be thinking in terms of similarities and differences. What do the two issues share in common, and what features of each are distinct? One approach might be to work first through all the similarities and then through all the contrasts (or vice versa). Another approach would be to discuss a similarity and contrast, followed by another similarity and contrast, etc.

Example – compare and contrast the uses of tea and coffee as beverages

Similarities

- Usually drunk hot
- Can be drunk with or without food
- Can be drunk with milk
- Can be taken with honey, sugar or sweeteners
- Both contain caffeine
- Both can be addictive

Contrasts

- Differences in taste
- Tea perhaps preferred at night
- Differences in caffeine content
- Coffee sometimes taken with cream or whiskey

- Each perhaps preferred with different foods
- Coffee preferred for hangover

> When you compare and contrast, you should aim to discuss different schools of thought and illustrate how the arguments differ.

Whenever evaluation is requested

A worked example of evaluation – Zero Tolerance and Restorative Justice

A BCU Commander had deployed a zero tolerance policing strategy for young offenders. He had been using this method successfully for nearly two years. Initially, this approach demonstrated a rapid reduction in youth offending. However, he had observed recently that the recidivism rate had increased month on month. A neighbouring BCU had adopted a restorative approach to youth offending. This scheme had seen a steady reduction in youth offending with no recent increase. The restorative justice scheme is 'owned' by the community and is reliant upon partnership and victim participation. You must evaluate the zero tolerance strategy to ascertain why the recidivism rate as increased and is there anyway of improving the approach without compromising the successful aspects. You might want to review past features (retrospective), outline present features (perspective) and envisage positive future changes (prospective). You may want to consider that restorative justice approach may be a better alternative strategy. This model can help answer a question that asks you to evaluate some theory or concept in most areas of police theory. Some summary points to guide are presented below:

- Has the theory/concept stood the test of time?
- Is there a supportive evidence base that would not easily be overturned?
- Are there questionable elements that have been or should be challenged?
- Does more recent evidence point to a need for modification?
- Is the theory/concept robust and likely to be around for the foreseeable future?
- Could it be strengthened through being merged with other theories/concepts?

Write your own checklist on what you remember or understand about each of the following: 'Discuss', 'Compare and contrast', 'Evaluate' and 'Critique' (just a key word or two for each). If you find this difficult, then you should read the section again and then try the exercise

✓ ....

✓ ....

✓ ....

✓ ....

It should be noted that the words presented in the above examples might not always be the exact words that will appear on your exam script. For example, you might find 'analyse', or 'outline' or 'investigate' rather than 'critique', 'discuss' or 'evaluate', etc. Check over past exam papers and familiarise yourself with the words that are most recurrent.

In summary, this chapter has identified reference points to measure where you are at in your studies, and to help you map out the way ahead in manageable increments. Learning is not merely a mechanical exercise, memorising and reproducing study material. *Quality learning involves making connections between ideas, thinking at a deeper level by attempting to understand the material and developing a critical approach to learning.* This cannot be achieved without the discipline of preparation for lectures, seminars and exams, or without learning to structure your material (headings and sub-headings) and to set each unit of learning within its overall context in your subject and programme. Develop the ability to ask questions (whether written, spoken or silent). Illustrate your material and use examples that will help make your study fun, memorable and vivid. Set problems for yourself that will allow you to think through solutions and therefore enhance the quality of your learning.

This chapter has presented strategies to help find the balance between organised and dynamic aspects of academic life: between the need to organise the material for easy retention, access and revision and the need to develop personal qualities such as feeding your confidence, fuelling your motivation and turning stress responses to your advantage.

The aim is to become an 'all round student', engaging in and benefiting from all the learning activities available to you (lectures, seminars, tutorials, computing, labs, discussions, library work, etc.), and developing all the academic and personal skills that will secure academic achievement. Recognising the value of these qualities, both across your academic programme and beyond graduation into the world of work will be motivating and build confidence. They will also serve you well in your continued commitment to life-long learning.

Textbook guide

BOOTH W ET AL. (2003) *The Craft of Research, Chicago: University of Chicago Press*
MCILROY D (2003) *Studying at University: How To Be a Successful Student, London: Sage*

part four

additional resources

4.1

Glossary, abbreviations and useful websites

This Glossary defines terms and explains abbreviations used in the book, and also provides useful websites where appropriate to supplement the entries.

ACPO	Association of Chief Police Officers in England, Wales and Northern Ireland. Representative body for chief constables, deputy chief constables, assistant chief constables and equivalent police staff roles. www.acpo.police.uk/
ACPO(S)	Association of Chief Police Officers in Scotland. Representative body for chief constables, deputy chief constables, assistant chief constables and equivalent police staff roles. www.scottish.police.uk/main/acpos/acpos.htm
APA	Association of Police Authorities www.apa.police.uk
APPRO	Association of Police Public Relations Officers http://appro.org.uk/
ASBO	Anti-Social Behaviour Order. Issued for a minimum of two years, ASBOs are court orders prohibiting the subject from certain behaviour, associating with certain people or visiting certain areas. The aim is to protect the public from offensive behaviour rather than punish the subject. Although an ASBO is a civil order, breach is a criminal offence. Police, local authorities and certain housing providers can apply for an ASBO to be issued. www.homeoffice.gov.uk/anti-social-behaviour/ www.homeoffice.go.uk/rds/pdfs2/hors236.pdf

Audit Commission   A non-departmental public body established in 1982 to conduct audits of local government public sector organisation efficiency and effectiveness. It published a series of influential reports on the police service in the late 1980s and early 1990s within the context of New Public Management. (The National Audit Office inspects central government.)
www.audit-commission.gov.uk/

BAWP   British Association of Women Police
www.bawp.org

BCU (a.k.a. OCU)   Basic Command Unit (or Borough Command Unit in the Metropolitan Police Service; Operational Command Unit in the West Midlands). The sub-force level, local administrative area of policing delivery. Each BCU is usually commanded by a chief superintendent or superintendent, and may itself be divided into smaller districts headed by chief inspectors or inspectors. BCUs are seen as the keystone to policing provision, and therefore of greater significance than forces, in Home Office (2004) *Beating Crime, Building Communities*, Cm 6360, London: HMSO, online at http://police.homeoffice.gov.uk/police-reform/white-paper.hmtl/?version=3

British Crime Survey   A biannual survey of victims against which to benchmark crime reported to the police. The survey reveals how much crime has not been reported to the police and provides an indication of the level of fear of crime.
www.homeoffice.gov.uk/rds/bcs1.html

BPA   National Black Police Association for black officers and police staff.
www.nationalbpa.com

BTP   British Transport Police. A non-Home Office force responsible for policing the British railway network.
www.btp.police.uk

CCTV	Closed-circuit television.
CDRP	Crime and Disorder Reduction Partnership. Partnerships between the police, local authorities and other partners (as required) to conduct local crime audits and devise community safety strategies. See crime and Disorder Act 1998, as amended by s. 97 Police Reform Act 2002.
Centrex	Central Police Training and Development Authority, established 2001, replacing the former National Police Training organisation. www.centrex.police.uk
CEOPS	Child Exploitation and Online Protection Centre, established 2006. www.ceop.gov.uk
Community Impact Assessment	Assessment of the impact that a significant incident or event will have on communities. The impact of an incident is dependent upon a range of factors, including the interrelationships that may exist between the different strata that make up a community, thus creating a range of potential hubs in which impacts and tensions may develop and emerge.
CPIA	Criminal Procedure and Investigation Act 1996. Law governing pre-trial disclosure of evidence, intended to ensure defendants have access to all relevant evidence. www.uk-legislation.hmso.gov.uk/acts/acts1996/1996025.htm
Critical incident management	Incidents where the effectiveness of the police response is likely to have a significant impact on the confidence of the victim, their family and/or the community. They can be characterised by fast-time pressure, incomplete information and rapidly changing circumstances and are complex to manage because of the challenging, uncertain and untested environment in which they occur.

Crown Prosecution Service	Public prosecutor agency in England and Wales, established 1986. www.cps.gov.uk
Desborough Committee	Established in March 1919 by the Home Office, chaired by Lord Desborough, to examine and make recommendations about police pay and service conditions following the police strike of 1918.
ECHR	European Convention on Human Rights and Fundamental Freedoms, Council of Europe, 1950. International foundation for the Human Rights Act 1998. www.echr.info See also www.echr.coe.int – European Court of Human Rights
EU	European Union http://europa.eu
Eurojust	An EU institution located in The Hague, it serves to channel information exchange and provide mutual legal assistance support to prosecutors in joint operations involving two or more EU member states. www.eurojust.eu.int
Europol	An EU institution located in The Hague, it serves to channel information exchange and provide intelligence support to investigators in joint operations involving two or more EU member states. www.europol.eu.int
Exculpatory evidence	Evidence that tends to prove the accused's innocence.
Extradition	A process of formal deportation, sending a suspect to a foreign jurisdiction where he or she is to stand trial for offences in the foreign jurisdiction.

FSS	Forensic Science Service www.fss.org.uk
GBH	Grievous bodily harm – criminal serious injury contrary to Offences Against the Person Act 1861
GMP	Greater Manchester Police www.gmp.police.uk
Green Paper	Government policy proposals published for public debate.
HMCE/HMRC	HM Customs and Excise, merged with the Inland Revenue (2005) to form HM Revenue and Customs. HMCE used to investigate organised crime concerning the importation of illicit goods. This function has now merged with SOCA. www.hmrc.gov.uk
HMIC	Her Majesty's Inspectorate of Constabulary. Founded 1856, HMIC conducts individual force and thematic inspections of policing on behalf of the Home Office. http://inspectorates.homeoffice.gov.uk/hmic/
HMIS/IND	HM Immigration Service, part of the Immigration and Nationality Directorate of the Home Office. That element of HMIS assigned to investigating organised human trafficking and large-scale illegal immigration has now merged with SOCA. www.ind.homeoffice.gov.uk
HOLMES	Home Office Large Major Enquiry System. Computerised evidence management system to assist in large-scale investigations. Updated recently as HOLMES2 www.holmes2.com/holmes2/index.php
Home Office	Government department with responsibility for policing, prisons, probation and immigration. Home Office police-related research is available at www.homeoffice.gov.uk/rds/index.htm

HRA	Human Rights Act 1998. Gives domestic effect to UK obligations under the ECHR. www.uk.legislation.hmso.gov.uk/acts/acts1998/19980042.htm
ICC	International Criminal Court www.icc-cpi.int
Inter alia	A common Latin term used by lawyers until the recent drive away from archaic court language, the meaning of which is 'among others'. Students will encounter its use in even quite recent law texts.
Interpol	Established in 1923, reconstituted in 1956, it is a non-governmental association of police agencies. It has no operational powers and assists in information exchange between foreign agencies. www.interpol.int
IPCC	Independent Police Complaints Authority. Established by the Police Reform Act 2002, it replaced the Police Complaints Authority. www.ipcc.gov.uk
JIT	Joint Investigation Team. A formal collaborative mechanism established in an EU inter-governmental treaty. It enables investigators/prosecutors from one state to work alongside foreign colleagues in that foreign jurisdiction.
JP	Justice of the Peace
LAGPA	Lesbian and Gay Police Association http://www.gay.police.uk/
Lyon Group	Group of law enforcement experts formed to advise G8 ministers and heads of government. It has various sub-groups, including one for hi-tech crime, the recommendations from which directly informed the establishment of NHTCU.

MI5 (Security Service)	Intelligence agency, part of the Civil Service, responsible for domestic (anti-terrorism, anti-extremism) security. It has a statutory remit to assist police in combating organised crime which it now fulfils by having contributed staff and resources to SOCA. www.mi5.gov.uk
MORI	Independent commercial market research company. www.mori.com
MPA	Metropolitan Police Authority. Established by the Greater London Authority Act 1999. Similar in function to police authorities elsewhere in England and Wales, the first public police authority for the MPS, which previously had been accountable directly to the Home Secretary. http://www.mpa.gov.uk/default.htm
MPS	Metropolitan Police Service. Founded 1829, it is responsible for policing those parts of London not policed by the City of London Police. It is the largest police force in UK. www.met.police.uk
Mutual legal assistance	Formal assistance mechanisms by which investigators in one national jurisdiction secure evidential assistance from authorities in a foreign state. http://police.homeoffice.gov.uk/operational-policing/mutual-legal-assistance/?version=2
NCIS	National Criminal Intelligence Service. Originally the National Drugs Intelligence Unit, located within the Home Office, it became an independent body on 1 April 1998 (established by the Police Act 1997), and merged into SOCA on 1 April 2006. www.ncis.gov.uk

NCPE

National Centre for Policing Excellence. Part of Centrex, it was established to develop police doctrine. It will be incorporated into the National Police Improvement Agency.

NCS

National Crime Squad. Established by the Police Act 1997, comprising the merger of the six Regional Criminal Squads, it became operational from 1 April 1998, and itself merged into SOCA on 1 April 2006.
www.nationalcrimesquad.police.uk

NHTCU

National Hi-Tech Crime Unit. A multi-agency unit comprising investigators from NCS, NCIS, HMCE and the RAF, hosted by NCS. Launched on 18 April 2001, it merged into SOCA on 1 April 2006.
www.nhtcu.org

NIM

National Intelligence Model. Established in 2000 to aid the prioritisation of law enforcement interventions.
www.police.uk/nim2

NPIA

National Police Improvement Agency. Innovation proposed in the Police Bill, 2006. It is intended to co-ordinate all aspects of improving policing. It will incorporate Centrex and its component parts, PITO, and the Home Office Police Standards Unit.
http://police.homeoffice.gov.uk/police-reform/reform-programme/national-policing-improvement/

NSLEC

National Specialist Law Enforcement Centre. Part of Centrex, it was responsible for training specialist investigation and intelligence skills.

OCU

See BCU

New Public Management

A 1980s philosophy that encouraged private sector approaches to managing public sector organisations.

PACE   Police and Criminal Evidence Act 1984. Statutory foundation for overt investigation powers such as arrest, stop and search, and interviewing. (The PACE Act is not available online.)

PCSO   Police community support officers. Non-sworn police staff undertaking uniform patrols for public re-assurance. They have limited enforcement powers. Alternatively termed community police support officers (CPSOs).

PIRA   Provisional Irish Republican Army, also known as the IRA. Irish nationalist terrorist organisation. PIRA is used to distinguish this principal movement from breakaway factions such as 'Continuity IRA' and the 'Real IRA'.

PITO   Police Information and Technology Organisation. Established in the Police Act 1997. To be merged into NPIA.
                www.pito.org.uk

Police   www.police.uk
                Relevant online legislation includes:
                Police Act 1996
                www.uk-legislation.hmso.gov.uk/acts/acts2000/20000023.htm
                Police Act 1997
                www.uk-legislation.hmso.gov.uk/acts/acts1997/1997050.htm
                Criminal Justice and Police Act 2001
                http://www.uk-legislation.hmso.gov.uk/acts/acts2001/20010016.htm
                Police Reform Act 2002
                http://www.uk-legislation.hmso.gov.uk/acts/acts2002/20020030.htm
                At the time of writing a Police and Justice Bill is currently being debated and, if enacted, is likely to become law in late 2006 or 2007.

Police Federation	Staff association for police officers in the ranks Constable up to chief inspector. www.polfed.org
Police Superintendents' Association	Staff association for police superintendents and chief superintendents www.policesupers.com
Probative value	Different forms of evidence proving a criminal charge carry different weight. Direct evidence, for example, is generally of greater probative value than circumstantial evidence.
Procurator Fiscal	The public prosecutor in Scotland. www.crownoffice.gov.uk
Protective services	A label used to describe a particular group of policing activities that generally transcend force boundaries or else often necessitate inter-force co-operation because individual forces do not have the resources to undertake the tasks effectively. Protective services comprise:

- Major crime (homicide)
- Serious, organized and cross-border crime
- Counter terrorism and extremism
- Civil contingencies
- Critical incidents
- Public order
- Strategic roads policing

HMIC thematic report *Closing the Gap* (2005) argues that force amalgamation is the only effective way to provide policing protective services. The APA disagrees, arguing that collaboration (which has never previously been completely effective) is the way forward.
http://inspectorates.homeoffice.gov.uk/hmic/inspect_reports/thematic-inspections/closinggap05.pdf

PSNI (formerly RUC) Police Service of Northern Ireland. Northern Ireland was previously policed by the Royal Ulster Constabulary. The PSNI was established as part of the peace process.
www.psni.police.uk

RCS Regional Crime Squad. First established in 1965 as collaborative ventures to address criminality that crossed police force boundaries in England and Wales. Initially nine, later reduced to six. Amalgamated in 1998 to form NCS.

RIPA Regulation of Investigatory Powers Act 2000. Law providing police powers of covert investigation.
www.uk-legislation.hmso.gov.uk/acts/acts2000/20000023.htm

Royal Commission Specific examinations of and inquiries into significant matters of (strategic) policy. Commissioners are appointed by the Crown for the purpose of the inquiry and usually have powers to call witnesses, require written submissions and examine all necessary documents and records.

SDEA Scottish Drug Enforcement Agency. Set up in June 2000 to investigate organised crime relating to drugs, this agency has not merged with SOCA and remains operational.
www.sdea.police.uk

SOCA Serious Organised Crime Agency. Established on 1 April 2006 by the SOCAP Act 2005.
www.soca.gov.uk

SOCAP Serious Organised Crime and Police Act 2005. Law founding SOCA and significantly amending PACE.
www.uk-legislation.hmso.gov.uk/acts/acts2005/20050015.htm

Statewatch An independent group monitoring the state and civil liberties in the UK and Europe and an excellent source for relevant original material for and commentary on police studies and related matters. It publishes a bi-monthly bulletin and has a very useful online subscription database. www.statewatch.org

UK   United Kingdom. UK legislation since 1988 is available online at www.uk-legislation.hmso.gov.uk/acts.htm

UN   United Nations

USA   United States of America

White Paper   Statements of government policy, such as plans for new legislation.

4.2

acts and documents relevant to the constitution of policing in england and wales

This table provides a chronological framework to help your understanding of the development of policing and the police service in England and Wales. Its focus is upon the *constitutional position* of policing rather than the practice or the sociology of policing, each of which deserve a similar table in their own right but is beyond the scope of this volume.

Acts in bold are of particular significance in the constitutional history of English policing, and are Acts the titles and years of which students should be able to cite in an exam/essay. Shaded Statutes distinguish between statutes and strategic documents.

Statute	Year	Provisions
Statute of Winchester	1285	Establishes, in statute, the principle of community self-policing. Norwich Chronicler: 'new statutes … against thieves, road brigands, receivers and concealers of malefactors, about setting watches in the country and townships and cities and the cutting away of woods by the King's highways.'
Justices of the Peace Act	1361	Local knights and gentry appointed to assist the sheriff, bailiffs and constables in the counties and hundreds in their enforcement duties to take up the 'hue and cry' and imprison suspects.
13 & 14 Charles II, Ch.12	1662	Created role of **special constables**, (a.k.a. parish Constables) to assist local Justices of the Peace.
Westminster Watch Act	1735	Parishes of St James, Piccadilly, and St George, Hanover Square, jointly obtain Act to improve their night watch provision. Five more parishes had adopted similar measures by 1736: an illustration of parishes taking responsibility for their own policing.
London and Westminster Police Bill	1785	Introduced by Pitt. Aborted. Aroused fears of French-style (political) policing, perceived as a threat to English liberties.

Statute	Year	Provisions
Dublin Police Act	1786	Revised version of the above, instituted in Ireland.
Middlesex Justices Act	1792	Set up seven police offices, each with three stipendiary magistrates and six constables. Origin of the Bow Street Runners. Over 300 constables so employed by 1828.
Thames Police Act	1800	Government assumed control of a private police force set up in 1798 by stipendiary magistrate Patrick Colquhorn.
Nightly Watch Regulation Bill	1812	Bill aborted because of continuing fears about French/Napoleonic style centralisation of policing. Parishes in particular opposed this Bill on the grounds that it threatened local control of the Watch and policing.
Metropolitan Police Act	**1829**	Established the Metropolitan Police (Service) headed by two Commissioners sworn in as magistrates, answerable to the Home Secretary and not the local community even though local authorities had to pay for the police force. A bone of contention, particularly as the new police force cost more than the Watch it replaced. Existed in parallel to Bow Street Runners established under the 1792 Act. The 1829 Act was silent on and therefore resolved none of the confusion surrounding the existence of two parallel policing organisations. Their functions overlapped, thus an opportunity was missed to have one organisation (the BSR) dedicated to detection and the other (MPS) dedicated to preventive patrol.
Cheshire Constabulary Act	1829	Provided for the appointment of a professional high constable in different hundreds in the county to liaise with urban police forces where these were established for the purpose of detecting and apprehending offenders. A very different model from the MPS model established in the same year.
Special Constables Act	1831	JPs empowered to conscript men as special constables on the occasion of a riot or threat of riot.
Lighting and Watching Act	1833	Provided framework for local authorities to improve day-time patrols and night watches. Entirely within the control of and answerable to local authorities.

Statute	Year	Provisions
Municipal Corporations Act	1835	Promoted uniformity of function among town councils, including a provision for the establishment of **Borough Watch Committees** which would appoint borough police forces. This provision was voluntary rather than mandatory. Applied to 178 boroughs in England and Wales of which about half had exercised the option to set up a Watch Committee by 1837. There was a considerable variety in the models of policing adopted. Prior to 1835, the appointment of JPs was a right granted by Royal Charter. This Act now required JPs to be nominated for each borough by the Lord Chancellor in consultation with local advisers. Outside towns, for the county benches, the Lord Chancellor continued to confirm the nomination of the Lord Lieutenants, who individually devised the criteria by which they nominated JPs. Both styles were Crown appointments acting on the Lord Chancellor's advice. (Exceptionally, in Lancashire, both town and country magistrates were nominated by the Chancellor of the Duchy of Lancashire.)
(First) Royal Commission on Policing	1836	Established to review the provision of policing in the counties.
City of London Police Act	1839	Established City of London (CoL) police, its own enclave within the metropolis answerable to the Aldermen rather than the Home Secretary. The CoL had fiercely defended its political autonomy from the metropolis and from the City of Westminster.
Metropolitan Police Act	1839	Put the magistracy in London on a proper statutory footing, providing court buildings maintained by the Receiver to the Metropolitan Police. As a result, for many years after this the courts were known as 'police courts', a description which has now fallen into disuse.
County Police Act a.k.a. Rural Police Act a.k.a. Rural Constabulary Act	**1839**	Outcome of the 1836 Royal Commission. It empowered county magistrates with determining whether or not to establish a rural police force within the county. It led to the reform of the police in the counties, driven by the need to maintain public order. Proposals were initially rejected by the Quarter Sessions, then accepted in the face of Chartist unrest. Take-up was initially voluntary. By 1856, when the County and Borough Police Act (see below) made rural police forces mandatory, only 25 out of 55 counties had installed police forces pursuant to the permissive legislation in the County Police Act.

Statute	Year	Provisions
		It was undermined by the fact that un-policed urban areas provided criminals with the opportunity to congregate with impunity. The Quarter Sessions [county courts] (until 1888) and Standing Joint Committee (SJC) (from 1889) were charged with appointing a chief constable. Once appointed the chief constable had great powers over the force and the SJC's powers were minimal. *[see Parish Constables Act 1842]*
Birmingham Police Act Bolton Police Act Manchester Police Act	1839	These Acts sought to take away control from the local authority and establish MPS-style policing models. Enacted at the time of Chartist unrest when the MPS was being drafted into Birmingham to subdue Chartist riots.
County Police Act	1840	Amended the 1839 Act by declaring that police forces established under the 1833 Lighting and Watching Act should be disestablished upon a county chief constable assuming responsibility for policing any district where such forces existed.
Parish Constables Act a.k.a Parochial Constables Act	**1842**	Provided an alternative policing model to that provided by the 1839 County Police Act. Required local magistrates to compile lists of rate-payers suitable for being sworn as constables. Preferred in many areas to the 1839 model of the county police force because it provided a more local policing solution. These (rate-payer) constables were to be supervised by a Superintending Constable.
Superintending Constables Act	1850	Revised arrangements for the appointment of Superintending Constables by providing that the Quarter Sessions could appoint such an officer (to oversee parish constables appointed pursuant to the 1842 Act) for any Petty Sessional District in the county.
(Second) Royal Commission on Policing	1855	Established to review complaints against the Metropolitan Police.
County and Borough Police Act	**1856**	Overturned the County Police Act *1839* by making the establishment of police forces mandatory. Such forces to be controlled by local authorities. Created the **HMIC** (whose evolution continued in s. 38 Police Act 1964 and s. 54 *Police Act* 1996) as a central mechanism for influencing and co-ordinating delivery of local policing. Forces identified as efficient by the HMIC would receive government grants.

Statute	Year	Provisions
		This legislation was resisted by local authorities (on the grounds that such central influence was anathema to English traditions of liberty and local control) until the Home Office increased the grant that would be payable to local forces identified as efficient by HMIC.
Police (Expenses) Act	1874	Increased the Exchequer grant to one-half the cost of police pay and clothing.
Municipal Corporation (New Charters) Act	1877	Prohibited the creation of new police forces for boroughs of less than 20,000 population.
Local Government Act	1888	Abolished existing police forces in boroughs of less than 10,000 population, reducing the number of forces in England and Wales from **231** to **183**. Left control of borough police forces in the hands of Watch Committees. Established **Police authorities** on the Standing Joint Committee model comprising 50% magistrates and 50% local councillors.
Police Act	1890	Established a pension after 25 years of service (or 15 if medically retired). Makes payment of Home Office grant subject to further conditions which included management and efficiency requirements.
Third) Royal Commission on Policing	1906	A further review of the handling of complaints against the Metropolitan Police.
Desborough Committee Report Part I, Part II	1919, 1920	Committee established to review recruiting, conditions of service and pay following police strikes in 1918 and 1919. Recommended improvement of pay and conditions to raise the status of constable from the equivalent of an agricultural labourer to that of a semi-skilled worker. Need for educated constables recognised. Recommended the creation of a Police Department within the Home Office; the abolition of borough forces serving a population of less than 50,000; the merger of smaller forces into regional entities overseen by a single chief officer and SJC (noting that a number of forces already shared a chief officer); and a uniform system of training to overcome anomalies of local variation between forces. Noted limited support for the proposal that the Criminal Investigation Department (CID) should be reconstituted as a national agency rather than be the responsibility of local forces.

Statute	Year	Provisions
Police Act	1919	Implemented many of Desborough's recommendations. Introduced limited supervision by the Home Secretary over conditions of service. Established the **Police Federation** and prohibited union membership for police officers. Widened the police services eligible for government grant.
Emergency Powers Act	1920	Allowed Executive to make 'regulations for the preservation of the public peace'. Home Secretary could direct mutual aid or police movements for any purpose.
(Fourth) Royal Commission on Policing	1929	Established to review police powers and procedures as defined in Judges Rules (first devised in 1912). Noted that the police, in exercising their functions, were 'to a peculiar degree', dependent upon public goodwill. Called for an increase in the number of policewomen.
Police Act	1946	Following amalgamation of 26 southern police forces during the Second World War as a measure to enhance co-ordination of effort in areas most threatened with invasion [*Defence (Amalgamation of Police Forces) Regulations 1942*], this Act brought about further amalgamations across the country, reducing the number of forces to **131**.
Miscellaneous Financial Provisions Act	1950	Empowered the Home Secretary to make conditions for payment of the 50% police grant.
(Fifth) Royal Commission on Policing	1960–62	Re-examined the fundamental principles of policing. A response to post-war increases in crime and road traffic problems; low police morale; (media-fuelled) concern about degenerating police/public relations; parliamentary frustration at having no influence over policing. Majority rejection of a national police force, with one Commissioner (Dr A L Goodhart) appending a dissenting conclusion in favour of a national police force. Other recommendations (inter alia): stronger central control in the hands of the Home Secretary; repeated Desborough's call for better-educated officers; merging Watch Committees and SJCs into new style Police Authorities, and removing their financial autonomy.

Statute	Year	Provisions
Police Act	**1964**	Implemented many recommendations of the 1960–62 Royal Commission.
		Repealed much of the nineteenth-century legislation structuring the police service, including abolition of the non-county borough as a police authority (with two exceptions).
		Established standard **police authorities** across the country, responsible for establishing an 'adequate and efficient' police force for their area.
		Supervisory power of Home Secretary enhanced: can call for reports and has oversight for police efficiency.
		Established power of Home Secretary to amalgamate force areas which the Home Secretary Roy Jenkins began to use in 1966, imposing force amalgamations in the face of local opposition in some cases. Reduced the number of police forces in England and Wales to **44** outside London.
Local Government Act	1972	As a result of the *Royal Commission on Local Government* (1966–69), further amalgamations reduced provincial forces to **41** in number, with two further forces serving London as all county boroughs were abolished and county councils were reduced from 58 to 47.
Police Act	1976	Established the **Police Complaints Board**; the first attempt to bring civilian oversight of complaints against police.
Local Government Act	1982	Created **Audit Commission** to inspect financial well-being of public sector organisations, including the police service (remit subsequently refined by later legislation).
Inquiry into Police Responsibilities and Rewards (Sir Patrick Sheehy) Cm 2280	June 1993	Wide-ranging reform proposed of rank structure, pay and conditions of the police service.
		Following outcry by police service, Home Secretary, having initially welcomed and endorsed this report, shelved it in October 1993.
Police Reform (White Paper) Cm 2281	1993	Resurrected some aspects of Sheehy. Suggested reform of police authorities.

Statute	Year	Provisions
Police and Magistrates Court Act	**1994**	Amended the Police Act 1964 redefining the functions and structures of police authorities (to include 'independent' members as well as councillors and JPs) and the functions of the Home Secretary within the tripartite relationship.
		Second Reading debate: Home Secretary stressed that the Bill focused on modernisation, reducing central accountability and increasing local accountability.
		Police Authorities to determine **local objectives** having regard for objectives set by Home Secretary and to publish **local policing plans** (s. 4).
		Preserved the power of Home Secretary to alter any police areas (other than that for the City of London) by order (s. 14).
		Home Secretary empowered to set **performance targets** (s. 15).
		Abolished deputy chief constable rank and reduced ranks between inspector and assistent chief constable to two.
Police Act	1996	A consolidation Act bringing together and making more readily accessible the existing law in relation to the organisation and administration of the police at the time to be found in the Police Act 1964 as amended by the Police and Magistrates Court Act 1994. Replaces the 1964 Act as amended.
The Role and Responsibilities of the Police (Ingrid Posen)	1996	Independent inquiry established by the Police Foundation and the Policy Studies Institute.
		Commissioned because of the adverse response to Sheehy. Focused on functions to ascertain how many could be delegated elsewhere. Concluded that relatively few could.
Police Act	**1997**	Part I Established **NCIS.**
		Part II Established **NCS.**
		Both funded by levy on police forces.
Crime and Disorder Act	1998	Statutory emphasis given to partnership working: **Crime and Disorder Strategies** are required by law; local Crime and Disorder Reduction Partnerships (**CDRPs**) are set up.
Local Government Act	1999	Establishes obligation on local authorities, including police service, to achieve 'best value'.

Statute	Year	Provisions
Policing a New Century: A Blue-print for Reform (Cm 5326)	Dec 2001	Emphasised importance of BCU in delivering local policing. Invited forces and police authorities to consider either more collaboration or further force amalgamations in order to achieve more effective policing provision. (**Police Standards Unit** set up as an internal department within the Home Office.)
Criminal Justice and Police Act	2001	Part IV reconstituted National Police Training as the Central Police Training and Development Authority (Centrex). Part V established the constitution of Police Authorities (including political balance). Sections 112 and 114 relate to the direct funding for NCIS and NCS.
Police Reform Act	2002	Part I – Home Secretary to produce a **National Policing Plan**. Part II – **IPCC** set up. Part III – outlines discipline measures for senior officers and Special Constables. Part IV Ch 1 – police powers to be held by civilians (**police-community support officers**, civilian crime investigators). s. 92 – Police authorities are required to produce three-year strategic plans. s. 97 – Amendments to the functions of CDRPs.
Policing: Building Safer Communities Together (Green Paper)	2003	Forerunner to November 2004 White Paper.
One Step Ahead: a 21st Century Strategy to Defeat Organised Crime (White Paper) Cm 6167	March 2004	Proposes the establishment of SOCA (to replace the NCIS and NCS), and enhancement of powers to investigate organised crime and seize criminal assets.
Policing: Modernising Police Powers to Meet Community Needs (Green Paper)	August 2004	Proposed redefining arrest powers and search warrant mechanisms (subsequently included in SOCAP Bill). Workforce modernisation, including expansion of police staff – enhanced powers for PCSOs proposed (again subsequently included in SOCAP Bill).

Statute	Year	Provisions
Managing Police Performance: A Practical Guide to Performance Management (Home Office guide to police forces)	September 2004	Produced by the Home Office Police Standards Unit and Accenture. It required forces to work to the **Police Performance Assessment Framework (PPAF)** which measures and compares strategic performance in policing provision. HMIC to conduct **baseline assessments** of 27 policing activity areas within individual forces. A manifestation putting Tony Blair's vision and four principles of public sector reform into action for the police service:increased flexibility; greater delegation and devolution to the front line; underpinned by accountability; and delivering improved performance.
Building Communities, Beating Crime: A better Police Service for the 21st Century (White Paper) Cm 6360	November 2004	Built on 2001 White Paper. It formally commissioned the HMIC to examine whether the police service is 'fit for purpose', the review having been actually commissioned in July 2004 by the Home Secretary's email to HM Chief Inspector of Constabulary. It re-emphasised the significance of the BCU and role the of the BCU commander, calling for formal vocational qualifications for BCU commanders.
Serious Organised Crime and Police Act	2005	Abolished the NCS and NCIS, also the investigation arms of HMCE and HMIS, to by replaced be the SOCA. Sought to create a new organisation with policing functions but which is not a police force, controlled by a Board of Directors. Staff will be designated with the powers of constable but will not be attested and will not hold the office of constable. Amended police and PCSO powers.
Closing the Gap – HMIC	September 2005	Questioned the extent to which the current 43-force structure is 'fit for purpose', particularly in relation to the delivery of **protective services**: • Major crime (homicide) • Serious, organised and cross-border crime • Counter terrorism and extremism • Civil contingencies • Critical incidents • Public order • Strategic roads policing

Statute	Year	Provisions
		Called into question the experience and capability at ACPO level within the service providing evidence that skills profiles reveal serious deficiencies in ability at ACPO level in many forces.
		On the basis of this report the Government called upon all forces in England and Wales to collaborate on merger proposals. This received mixed response among forces and opposition from APA.
		With a change of Home Secretary, restructuring plans were indefinitely postponed in June 2006.
		The serious questions posed by *Closing the Gap* remain unanswered; the problems it identifies remain unresolved at time of writing.
Police and Justice Bill	2006	Proposes a new **National Police Improvement Agency** (NPIA) to consolidate functions currently undertaken by the Home Office Police Standards Unit, the National Centre for Policing Excellence, PITO, Centrex (formerly National Police Training), the Police Leadership and Powers Unit and aspects of HMIC's work.
		Proposes merging the current inspection bodies – HMIC, HMI Prisons, HMI National Probation Service, HMI Crown Prosecution Service and HMI Court Administration – into a single **HM Inspectorate for Justice, Community Safety and Custody**.
		Proposes establishing BCUs on a statutory footing, requiring them to be coterminous with local authority boundaries.
		Proposes amendments to the strategic powers of the Home Secretary, repealing requirement to issue a National Policing Plan, replacing it with a wider **Community Safety Plan**, but expanding the triggers that empower a Home Secretary to intervention in a 'failing' force.
		Proposes amendments to the police authorities with particular reference to improving consultation processes with the public (research having shown that engagement between authorities and the public – part of their *raison d'être* – is very poor), and to giving the Home Secretary greater powers and flexibility to alter the structure and functions of authorities.

4.3
references and additional reading

There follows a supplementary bibliography arranged by thematic section.

Key texts

Kennedy H (2004) *Just Law: The Changing Face of Justice – and Why It Matters To Us All*, London: Vintage

Maguire M, Reiner R & Morgan R (eds) (2002) *The Oxford Handbook of Criminology* (3rd edn), Oxford: Oxford University Press

McConville M & Wilson G (eds) (2002) *The Handbook of the Criminal Justice Process*, Oxford: Oxford University Press

Newburn T (ed.) (2003) *Handbook of Policing*, Cullompton: Willan

Newburn T (ed.) (2005) *Policing: Key Readings*, Cullompton: Willan

Smartt U (2006) *Criminal Justice,* London: Sage

Although not a substitute for academic texts, it can be useful to read journalistic accounts aimed at the popular market to obtain a different perspective, one which the public is likely to adopt. For an account of investigating organised crime see:

Barnes T, Elias R & Walsh P (2000) *Cocky: The Rise and Fall of Curtis Warren, Britain's Biggest Drug Baron*, Bury: Milo Books

For a profoundly thought-provoking account of a victim's perspective of justice and the trial evidential process, see the Australian case study:

Garner H (2004) *Joe Cinque's Consolation: A True Story of Death, Grief and the Law*, Sydney: Picador

2.0 Running themes

Smartt U (2006) *Criminal Justice*, London: Sage

The policing framework

2.1 The emergence and history of policing

Ascoli D (1979) *The Queen's Peace: The Origins and Development of the Metropolitan Police 1829–1979*, London: Hamish Hamilton

Gaskill M (1996) 'The displacement of providence: policing and prosecution in seventeenth- and eighteenth-century England', *Continuity and Change* 11, pp. 347–74.

Home Office (2004) *One Step Ahead: A 21st Century Strategy to Defeat Organised Crime*, Cm 6167, London: TSO

HMIC (2005) *Closing the Gap: A Review of the 'Fitness for Purpose' of the Current Structure of Policing in England and Wales*, London: Home Office

Hudson J (1996) *The Formation of the English Common Law: Law and Society in England from the Norman Conquest to Magna Carta*, Oxford: Oxford University Press

Kent J (1986) *The English Village Constable, 1580–1642: A Social and Administrative Study*, Oxford: Oxford University Press

Rawlings P (1996) 'The idea of history: a history', *Policing and Society* 5 pp. 129–49

Stallion M & Wall D (1999) *The British Police: Police Forces and Chief Officers 1829–2000*, Bramshill: Police History Society

2.2 The function and role of the police

Alderson J (1979) *Policing Freedom: A Commentary on the Dilemmas of Policing in Western Democracies*, Plymouth: Macdonald & Evans

Garland D (2001) *The Culture of Control*, Oxford: Oxford University Press

Johnston L (2000) *Policing Britain: Risk, Security and Governance*, Harlow: Longman

Jones T & Newburn T (1997) *Policing after the Act: Police Governance after the Police and Magistrates Court Act*, London: Policy Studies Institute

Mawby R (2002) *Policing Images*, Cullompton: Willan

Newburn T (ed.) (2005) *Policing: Key Readings*, Cullompton: Willan (Part B)

Posen I (1996) *The Role and Responsibilities of the Police*, London: Police Foundation/Policy Studies Institute

Sheehy P (1993) *Inquiry into Police Responsibilities and Rewards*, Cm 2280, London: HMSO

Wright A (2002) *Policing: An Introduction to Concepts and Practice*, Cullompton: Willan

2.3 Governance, structure and accountability

Harfield C (2006) 'SOCA: a paradigm shift in British policing', *British Journal of Criminology* 46 (4), pp. 743–71

HMIC (2005) *Closing the Gap: A Review of the 'Fitness for Purpose' of the Current Structure of Policing in England and Wales* London: Home Office

Home Office (2004) *One Step Ahead: A 21st Century Strategy to Defeat Organised Crime,* Cm 6167, London: TSO

Jones T & Newburn T (1997) *Policing after the Act: Police Governance after the Police and Magistrates Court Act 1994,* London: Policy Studies Institute

Loveday B (2000) 'New directions in accountability', in F Leishman et al. (eds), *Core Issues in Policing,* Harlow: Longman, pp. 213–31

Reiner R (1991) *Chief Constables,* Oxford: Oxford University Press

Reiner R (2000) *The Politics of the Police* (3rd edn) Oxford: Oxford University Press

Savage S et al. (2000) 'The policy-making in context: who shapes policing policy?', in F Leishman et al. (eds), *Core Issues in Policing,* Harlow: Longman, pp. 30–51

Wall D (1998) *The Chief Constables of England and Wales,* Aldershot: Dartmouth

2.4 Public engagement and the police

Alderson J (1977) *Communal Policing,* Exeter: Devon & Cornwall Constabulary

Farrell G & Pease K (2001) *Repeat Victimisation,* Monsey, NY: Criminal Justice Press

Home Office (2003) *The Role of Police Authorities in Public Engagement,* London: HMSO

Jones T et al. (1994) *Democracy and Policing,* London: Policy Studies Institute

Loader I & Mulcahy A (2003) *Policing and the Condition of England,* Oxford: Oxford University Press

Reiner R & Spencer S (eds) (1993) *Accountable Policing: Effectiveness, Empowerment and Equity,* London: Policy Studies Institute

2.5 Philosophies of policing – Keeping the peace and enforcing the law

Alderson J (1977) *Communal Policing,* Exeter: Devon & Cornwall Constabulary

Bayley D (1994) *Police for the Future,* New York: Oxford University Press

Brogdan M & Nijhar P (2005) *Community Policing,* Cullompton: Willan

Ericson R & Haggerty K (1997) *Policing the Risk Society*, Oxford: Oxford University Press

Goldstein H (1990) *Problem-oriented Policing*, New York: McGraw-Hill (originally published 1979)

Hale C et al. (2004) 'Uniform styles? Aspects of police centralization in England and Wales', *Policing & Society* 14 (4), pp. 291–312

Hale C et al. (2005) 'Uniform Styles II: police families and policing styles', *Policing & Society* 15 (1), pp. 1–18

Home Office (2004) *Building Communities, Beating Crime: A Better Police Service for the 21st Century*, Cm 6360, London: HMSC.

Maguire M (2003) 'Criminal investigation and crime control', in T Newburn (ed.), *Handbook of Policing*, Cullompton: Willan, pp. 363–93

2.6 Comparative policing

Anderson D & Killingray D (eds) (1991) *Policing the Empire*, Manchester: Manchester University Press

Anderson D & Killingray D (eds) (1992) *Policing and Decolonisation*, Manchester: Manchester University Press

Brodeur J-P (1995) *Comparisons in Policing: An International Perspective*, Aldershot: Avebury

Findlay M & Zvekic U (eds) (1993) *Alternative Policing Styles: Cross-Cultural Perspectives*, Boston: Kluwer.

Horton C (1995) *Policing Policy in France*, London: Policy Studies Institute

Mawby R (1990) *Comparative Policing Issues*, London: Unwin Hyman

Mawby R (1999) *Policing across the World: Issues for the 21st Century*, London: UCL Press

Mawby R (2003) 'Models of Policing', in T Newburn (ed.), *Handbook of Policing*, Cullompton: Willan, pp. 15–40

Shelley L (1996) *Policing Soviet Society*, London: Routledge

2.7 International and transnational policing

Cullen P & Gilmore W (eds) (1998) *Crime Sans Frontières: International and European Legal Approaches*, Edinburgh: Edinburgh University Press

Harfield C (2002) 'Issues in transatlantic policing' *The Police Journal* 75 (3), pp. 204–22

Hebenton B & Thomas T (1995) *Policing Europe: Co-operation, Conflict and Control*, Basingstoke: St Martin's Press

Koenig D & Das D (eds) (2001) *International Police Co-operation: A World Perspective*, Lanham, MD: Lexington Books

McDonald W (1997) *Crime and Law Enforcement in the Global Village*, Cincinnati: ACJS/Anderson

Occhipinti J (2003) *The Politics of EU Police Co-operation: Toward a European FBI?* Boulder, CO: Lynne Reiner

Williams P & Vlassis D (eds) (2001) *Combating Transnational Crime: Concepts, Activities and Responses*, London: Frank Cass

2.8 Partnership and police reform

Appleby P (1995) *A Force on the Move: The Story of the British Transport Police 1825–1995*, Malvern: Images

Barlow H & Murphy L (1997) *The History and Development of the Ministry of Defence Police from the 17th Century*, Wethersfield: MOD Police

HMIC (2005) *Closing the Gap*, London: HMIC

Home Office (2004b) *Building Communities, Beating Crime: A Better Police Service for the 21st Century*, Cm 6360, London: HMSO

Home Office (2004c) *One Step Ahead: A 21st Century Strategy to Defeat Organized Crime*, Cm 6167, London: HMSO

Home Office (2004) *Building Communities, Beating Crime: A Better Police Service for the 21st Century*. Cm 6360, London: TSO

Home Office (2004) *One Step Ahead; A 21st Century strategy to Defeat Organised Crime*, Cm 6167, London: TSO

Home Office 1993, *Police Reform: The Government's Proposals for the Police Service in England and Wales*, Cm 2281, London: HMSO

House of Commons Second Reading Debate on the Police Bill (Private Members), 19 February (1998) *Hansard*, cols 729–35

House of Commons Standing Committee D, 11 January 2005

House of Lords Select Committee on Unopposed Bills, Minutes of Evidence, 19 February 2003, paragraphs 600–19

Jones T & Newburn T (1998) *Private Security and Public Policing*, Oxford: Clarendon Press

Sir Ian Blair, 'What kind of police service do we want?' The 30th Richard Dimbleby Lecture, 16 November 2005, transcript available at http://news.bbc.co.uk/1/hi/uk/4443386.stm (accessed 22 February 2007).

The practice of policing

2.9 Policing public order

Campbell S (2002) *A Review of Anti-Social Behaviour Orders*, Home Office Research Study 236, London: Home Office, also online at www.homeoffice.go.uk/rds/pdfs 2/hors 236.pdf

Hughes G & Edwards A (2003) *Crime Control and Community: The New Politics of Public Safety*, Cullompton: Willan

Pattten C (1999) A New Beginning: Policing in Northern Ireland, Belfast: HMSO

Ridley N (1991) *My Style of Government*, London: Hutchinson

Waddington D (1998) 'Waddington vs Waddington: public order theory on trial', *Theoretical Criminology* 2 (3), pp. 373–94

2.10 Criminal investigation

Cheney D et al. (2001) *Criminal Justice and the Human Rights Act 1998*, Bristol: Jordans

English J & Card R (2005) *Police Law* (9th edn), Oxford: Oxford University Press

Mansfield M & Wardle T (1993) *Presumed Guilty: The British Legal System Exposed*, London: Heinemann

Newburn T et al. (2007) *Handbook of Criminal Investigation*, Cullompton: Willan

Zander M (2005) *The Police and Criminal Evidence Act* (5th edn), London: Sweet & Maxwell

2.11 Policing and evidence

Choo A (1998) *Evidence: Text and Materials*, Harlow: Longman

Mansfield M & Wardle T (1993) *Presumed Guilty: The British Legal System Exposed*, London: Heinemann

Ryan C, Savla S & Scanlan G (1996) *A Guide to the Criminal Procedure and Investigations Act 1996*, London: Butterworths

Sprack J (2006) *A Practical Approach to Criminal Procedure* (11th edn), Oxford: Oxford University Press

2.12 Policing different types of crime

Bean P (2002) *Drugs and Crime*, Cullompton: Willan

Braga A (2002), *Problem-oriented Policing and Crime Prevention*, Monsey, NY: Criminal Justice Press

Farrell G & Pease K (2001) *Repeat Victimisation*, Crime Prevention Studies Series 12, Monsey, NY: Criminal Justice Press

Garland D (2001) *The Culture of Control*, Oxford: Oxford University Press

Gregory J & Lees S (1999) *Policing Sexual Assault*, London: Routledge

Ruggiero V (2000) *Crime and Markets: Essays in Anti-Criminology*, Oxford: Oxford University Press

Temkin J (2002) *Rape and Legal Process*, Oxford: Oxford University Press

2.13 Policing organised crime

Berdal M & Serrano M (eds) (2002) *Transnational Organized Crime & International Security: Business as Usual?* Boulder, CO: Lynne Rienner

Harfield C (2006) 'SOCA: a paradigm shift in British policing', *British Journal of Criminology* 46 (4), pp. 743–71

Home Affairs Committee (1995) *Organized Crime*, Third Report (House of Commons Session 1994–95, 18–I)

Home Office (2004) *One Step Ahead: A 21st Century Strategy to Defeat Organized Crime*, Cm 6167, London: HMSO

Wright A (2005) *Organised Crime*, Cullompton: Willan

2.14 Policing cyberspace

Mansell R & Collins B (eds) (2005) *Trust and Crime in Information Societies*, Cheltenham: Edward Elgar

MacVean A & Spindler P (2003) *Policing Paedophiles on the Internet*, London: The New Police Bookshop

Stephenson P (2000) *Investigating Computer-related Crime*, New York: CRC Press

Stoll C (1989) *The Cuckoo's Egg: Tracking a Spy Through the Maze of Computer Espionage*, New York: Pocket Books

Sussman M (1999) 'The critical challenges from international high-tech and computer-related crime at the millennium', *Duke Journal of Comparative & International Law* 9 (2), pp. 451–89

2.15 Policing terrorism

Donohue L (2001) *Counter-terrorist Law and Emergency Powers in the United Kingdom 1922–2000*. Dublin: Irish Academic Press

Freedman L (ed.) (2002) *Superterrorism: Policy Responses*, Oxford: Blackwell

Ni Aolain F (2000) *The Politics of Force: Conflict Management and State Violence in Northern Ireland*, Belfast: Blackstaff

Independent Monitoring Commission Northern Ireland (2003–06) *Reports 1–12*, London: HMSO

Mulcahy A (2006) *Policing Northern Irland: Conflict, Legitimacy and Reform*, Cullompton: Willan

Van Leeuwen M (ed.) (2003) *Confronting Terrorism: European Experiences, Threat Perceptions and Policies*, The Hague: Kluwer Law International

2.16 Private policing

Crawford A, (2003) 'The pattern of policing in the UK: beyond the police' in Newburn T (ed.), *Handbook of Policing*, Cullompton: Willan, pp. 136–168.

Johnson L (1996) 'What is vigilantism?', *British Journal of Criminology* 36 (2), pp. 220–36

Kempa M, Carrier R, Wood J & Shearing C (1999) 'Reflections on the evolving concept of "private policing"', *European Journal on Criminal Policy and Research* 7 (2), pp. 197–223

Patten C (199) *A New Beginning: Policing in Northern Ireland*, Belfast: HMSO

Shearing C & Stenning P (eds) (1981) 'Modern private security: its growth and implications', *Crime and Justice* 3, pp. 193–24

South N (1988) *Policing for Profit*, London: Sage

The cultural context of policing

2.17 Police ethics and human rights

Ashworth A (2002) *Human Rights, Serious Crime and Criminal Procedure*, London: Sweet & Maxwell

Chan J (1997) *Changing Police Culture: Policing in a Multi-cultural Society*, Cambridge: Cambridge University Press

Feldman D (2002) *Civil Liberties and Human Rights in England and Wales* (2nd edn), Oxford: Oxford University Press (Parts I and II but particularly Chapter 6)

Garner H (2004) *Joe Cinque's Consolation: A True Story of Death, Grief and the Law*, Sydney: Picador

Kennedy H (2004) *Just Law: The Changing Face of Justice and Why It Matters To Us All*, London: Vintage

Kleinig J (1996) *The Ethics of Policing*, Cambridge: Cambridge University Press

Klockers C et al. (2003) *The Contours of Police Integrity*, London: Sage

Neyroud P (2003) 'Policing and ethics', in T Newburn (ed.), *Handbook of Policing*, Cullompton: Willan, pp. 578–602

Neyroud P & Beckley A (2001) *Policing, Ethics and Human Rights*, Cullompton: Willan

Starmer K (1999) *European Rights Law*, London: Legal Action Group

Starmer K et al. (2001) *Criminal Justice, Police Powers and Human Rights*, London: Blackstones

Wadham J & Mountfield H (1999) *Blackstone's Guide to The Human Rights Act 1998*, London: Blackstone

2.18 The organisational culture of the police

Chan J (1997) *Changing Police Culture: Policing in a Multi-cultural Society*, Cambridge: Cambridge University Press

Fielding N (1998) *Joining Forces: Police Training, Socialisation and Occupational Culture*, London: Routledge

Hobbs R (1988) *Doing the Business: Entrepreneurship, the Working Class, and Detectives in East London*, Oxford: Oxford University Press

Holdaway S (1983) *Inside the British Police*, Oxford: Blackwell

Hopkins-Burke R (2004) *Hard Cop, Soft Cop*, Cullompton: Willan

Newburn T (ed.) (2005) *Policing: Key Readings*, Cullompton: Willan (Part C)

Reiner R (2000) *The Politics of the Police* (3rd edn), Oxford: Oxford University Press

Scarman Lord (1981) *The Brixton Disorders 10–12 April 1981*, Cmnd 84–27, London: HMSI

Waddington P (1999) 'Police (canteen) sub-culture: an appreciation', *British Journal of Criminology* 39 (2), pp. 286–309

Wall D (1998) *The Chief Constables of England and Wales*, Aldershot: Dartmouth

2.19 Race and diversity

Fitzgerald M (1993) *Ethnic Minorities in the Criminal Justice System*, London: HMSO

Holdaway S & Barron A (1997) *Resigners? The Experience of Black and Asian Police Officers*, London: Macmillan.

Laming Lord (2003) *The Victoria Climbié Inquiry*, Cm 5730, London: HMSO

MacPherson W (1999) *The Stephen Lawrence Inquiry*, Cm 4262, London: HMSO

Morris W (2004) *The Case for Change: An Independent Inquiry in to Professional Standards and Employment Matters in the Metropolitan Police*, London: Metropolitan Police Authority

Patten C (1999) *A New Beginning: Policing in Northern Ireland*, Belfast: HMSO
Rowe M (2004) *Policing, Race and Racism*, Cullompton: Willan
Scarman Lord (1981) *The Brixton Disorders 10–12 April 1981*, Cmnd 8427, London: HMSO

2.20 Gender and policing

Brown J & Heidensohn F (2000) *Gender and Policing*, Basingstoke: Palgrave Macmillan
Gelsthorpe L (2002), 'Feminism and criminology', in M Maguire et al. (eds), *The Oxford Handbook of Criminology* (3rd edn), Oxford: Oxford University Press, pp. 112–43
Heidensohn F (1989) *Women in Policing in the USA*, London: Police Foundation
Heidensohn F (2000) *Sexual Politics and Social Control*, Buckingham: Open University Press
Lock J (1979) *The British Policewoman: Her Story*, London: Hale
Wyles L (1951) *A Woman at Scotland Yard*, London: Faber

2.21 The police and the media

Bailey F & Hale D (eds) (1998) *Popular Culture, Crime and Justice*, Belmont, CA: Wadsworth
Howitt S (1998) *Crime, the Media and the Law*, London: Wiley
Innes M (1999) 'The media as an investigative resource in murder enquiries', *British Journal of Criminology* 39 (2), pp. 268–85
Leishman F & Mason P (2003) *Policing and the Media: Facts, Fictions and Factions*, Cullompton: Willan
Reiner R (2002) 'Media made criminality', in M Maguire et al. (eds), *The Oxford Handbook of Criminology* (3rd edn), Oxford: Oxford University Press, pp. 376–416
Surette R (1998) *Media, Crime and Criminal Justice* (2nd end), Belmont, CA: Wadsworth

Academic skills

Cottrell S (2003) *The Study Skills Handbook*, Basingstoke: Palgrave Macmillan
Dunleavy P (1986) *Studying for a Degree in the Humanities and Social Sciences*, Milton Keynes: Open University Press

McIlroy D (2003) *Studying at University: How To Be a Successful Student*, London: Sage

Northedge A (2005) *The Good Study Guide*, Milton Keynes: Open University Press

Tracy E (2002) *The Students' Guide to Exam Success*, Basingstoke: Palgrave Macmillan

Academic Journals

Students should, as a matter of course, monitor academic journals for papers and articles of relevance to policing. There are a great many of these and what follows is just a sample representing the diversity of approaches that can be adopted when studying policing.

British Journal of Criminology
Crime, Law and Social Change
Crime Prevention and Community Safety
Criminal Justice
Criminal Justice Matters
Criminal Law
Criminal Law Review
Criminology and Public Policy
Critical Social Policy
Covert Policing Review
European Human Rights Law Review
European Journal of Crime, Criminal Law and Criminal Justice
European Journal of Criminology
European Journal on Criminal Policy and Research
Howard Journal of Criminal Justice
International and Comparative Law Quarterly
International Journal of Comparative & Applied Criminal Justice
International Journal of Police Science & Management
International Journal of the Sociology of Law
Journal of Criminal Justice
Journal of Criminal Law
Journal of Law and Society
Journal of Police Science and Administration
Police Journal
Policing
Policing and Society
Social and Legal Studies
Transnational Organized Crime

There are also the following relevant professional and journalistic periodicals

Criminal Justice Management
Police Professional
Police Review
Policing Today

index